Topics in Operational Research

A series of books under the advisory editorship of
Professor S. Vajda of the University of Birmingham

Basic Operational Research

Topics in Operational Research

Since the end of the Second World War, studies in the field of Management Sciences and Operational Research have developed at an extraordinary speed, and have gained in width and depth.

The present series of books on "Topics in Operational Research" contains contributions from authors who have special expertise in this field. There exist, of course, excellent texts on the theoretical background, but this series fulfils a need for detailed descriptions of simple numerical or algebraic techniques, and for reports on practical experience with these techniques, useful to managers and executives in many branches of social, commercial, and industrial activity. Knowledge of such techniques will be spread more widely by the publication of these monographs, and further development stimulated thereby.

The texts are written in such a way that little, if any, advanced knowledge from any branch of science or mathematics will be required of the reader.

The various books in the series should thus be of interest not only to management and engineering personnel, but also to teachers in the later forms in schools, and in colleges, as suggestions for possible syllabuses for introductory courses and as sources of interesting problems and examples.

S. VAJDA

Basic Operational Research

P. G. MOORE

Professor of Statistics
and Operational Research
London Graduate School
of Business Studies

London
Sir Isaac Pitman & Sons Ltd.

First Published 1968

SIR ISAAC PITMAN AND SONS LTD.
Pitman House, Parker Street, Kingsway, London, W.C.2
Pitman House, Bouverie Street, Carlton, Victoria 3053, Australia
P.O. Box 7721, Johannesburg, Transvaal, S. Africa
P.O. Box 6038, Portal Street, Nairobi, Kenya

PITMAN PUBLISHING CORPORATION
20 East 46th Street, New York, N.Y. 10017

SIR ISAAC PITMAN (CANADA) LTD.
Pitman House, 381–383 Church Street, Toronto

SBN: 273 42709 1

Made in Great Britain at the Pitman Press, Bath
(T.1146)

Preface

Some four years ago I gave a series of lectures on operational research to a summer school at an American university. The audience was mainly businessmen who wanted to get an understanding of this new, or relatively new, speciality that had sprung up in so many organizations. The discussions I had then first put the idea of writing the present book into my mind, but it was the experience of helping to set up the London Graduate School of Business Studies at the end of 1965 that confirmed me in the need for the book. At the School we have regular three-month executive courses for up-and-coming middle managers and one aim is to introduce the participants to specialities such as operational research, thereby improving their analytical skills, as well as their ability to recognize and formulate problems within a quantitative framework and to interpret the results. The need for some reference book to go with this series of classroom sessions was a compelling motive to go ahead with the book sketched out earlier.

The book has been written for two classes of reader. The first is the manager or executive mentioned above. The second is the more serious student who can use the book as an introduction to the subject before, or at the same time as, studying the more sophisticated texts that are available. The aim throughout has been to speak (or rather to write) through problems and to allow these to dictate the pace and the manner of approach. I suggest that this is valuable in providing a reference point for the majority of the readers I have in mind. Too many books for such readers seem to me to put all their primary effort into the middle, that is the black box, part of the subject and then to work backwards to the problem formulation stage and forwards to the solution interpretation stage. I have deliberately set out to start the discussions with recognizable problems, most of them real or adapted real ones, and to skate over much of the black box manipulations so as to come to grips reasonably quickly with the solution and its interpretation. Of course, I have found it necessary to keep to a framework that is broadly technique-based to provide an acceptable thread of continuity, and also an ease of consultation with the recognized formal texts on the subject.

Operational research is not a universal panacea. It is a serious attempt to bring scientific methods to the aid of business problems. A concise definition I give in the first chapter suggests that it is concerned with the allocation of scarce resources in complex and competing situations. Accepting this necessarily over-simplified definition implies that it must have a very definite relationship with many other subject areas, e.g. accountancy, economics, statistics, to name some of the obvious ones. This will become clear in the book, but what will also, I hope, become clear is the extra power, and indeed dimension, of problem analysis and resolution that is made available by precisely this combination of expertise. For those expecting a do-it-yourself kit there will be disappointment, but for those who want to learn something of the flavour and ethos of the subject, I hope there will be satisfaction.

The book, with its heavy emphasis on case histories and problems that have a real background, has necessarily drawn upon a variety of both published and unpublished sources and has quoted from many reports and journals. In most instances I have made only partial quotations, as the extract has been confined to illustrate particular points. Wherever the data are substantially in the original form, due acknowledgment has been made through the references appended to each chapter. These references will also enable the reader to pursue many of the case histories further, if he so desires. I must, however, in particular, make acknowledgment to the Ministry of Technology (and especially L. R. Carter and R. C. Johnson) for the original report on which the materials equipment problem in Chapter 4 is based; Her Majesty's Stationery Office for Figure 2.5 extracted from the publication quoted in Chapter 2; the American Marketing Association and Professor P. E. Green for some extracts on the plastics pricing problem in section 9.5; the Harvard Business Review for Figure 7.6 and some of the data in section 8.7; and Mr. P. Sandford-Johnson for the original data used in section 2.9. It is also a pleasure to acknowledge the help and encouragement received from many quarters in the preparation of the book. Stewart Hodges, my research assistant, read and commented on the entire manuscript, making many valuable suggestions. My secretary, Sheila Ewart, demonstrated abundant patience in producing order out of numerous piles of notes, and my wife has given me a great deal of help, particularly with the proof-reading. To all these people my grateful thanks are due. The shortcomings, errors, ambiguities, and obscurities that remain are all mine.

London, July 1968   P. G. M.

Contents

Preface   v

1 The Operational Research Approach   **1**
  1 Introduction   1
  2 The complexity of problems   2
  3 Essential characteristics   5
  4 Types of model   8
  5 The phases of the study   11
  6 Shipping channel illustration   13
  7 Form and content   15

2 The Programming of Resources—Networks   **18**
  1 Background   18
  2 The method   20
  3 Drawing the network   21
  4 Illustration   23
  5 The analysis of the network   25
  6 Forming a new organization   28
  7 Controlling the project   29
  8 Fitting out a hotel   31
  9 The cost of using network analysis   31

3 The Programming of Resources—The Graphical Approach to Allocation   **33**
  1 The wood-working business   33
  2 The general allocation problem   34
  3 The Transrad company   36
  4 Additional constraints   40
  5 Relaxation of constraints   42
  6 A minimum cost problem   44
  7 Power and limitations   45
  8 Linearity   47

4   The Programming of Resources—The Mathematical Approach to Allocation   **49**
1   The approach   49
2   A handling equipment problem   49
3   The basic data   50
4   The solution and its interpretation   52
5   Further implications   54
6   A problem in paper-making   55
7   The optimum solution   58
8   Planning over time   60

5   The Planning of Operations—Queueing   **62**
1   Introduction   62
2   Traffic intensity   64
3   The avoidance of bottlenecks   65
4   The servicing of machines   69
5   Generalization of servicing problem   71
6   Alternative analysis   73
7   Post Office counter problem   74

6   The Planning of Operations—Simulation   **77**
1   Introduction   77
2   The Monte Carlo technique   79
3   Drawing the sample   81
4   The rolling mill   83
5   The simulation model   85
6   Unloading at a port   85
7   General business simulation   88
8   Impact of simulation on management   89

7   Inventory and Stock Control   **91**
1   Introduction   91
2   The square-root formula   91
3   Sensitivity of the result   94
4   Re-order levels   96
5   Choice of buffer stock   97
6   Safety stocks and service   99
7   Centralized stores   100
8   Industrial dynamics   102
9   Inventory control systems   105
10 Feedback control systems   106

8 Decision Analysis **109**
1 Introduction 109
2 Maximin decision rule 110
3 Minimax regret rule 111
4 Installation of a boiler 112
5 Expected values 115
6 Concept of repeatability 116
7 The "dissolving" chemical company 118
8 The analysis of the problem 120
9 Risk aversion 125
10 General considerations 126

9 Some Further Operational Research Problems **128**
1 Introduction 128
2 Location problem 128
3 Capital budgeting procedures 132
4 Optimum media schedules 135
5 A pricing problem in plastics 138
6 The checking of invoices and bills 147

10 Implementation and the Future **152**
1 Comprehensive models 152
2 The variables included 154
3 Methods of solution 155
4 The importance of implementation 157
5 The role of operational research 160
6 Organization 162
7 The selection of personnel 165

Appendix A: The Simplex Method for Linear Programming **167**
1 Introduction 167
2 The simplex procedure 167
3 A graphical analysis 171
4 References to programming techniques 173

Appendix B: Some Statistical Concepts **175**
1 Inferential statistics 175
2 The sample 175
3 The accuracy of a proportion 177
4 The interpretation of a sampling distribution 178
5 The confidence interval 180

Index 183

1 The Operational Research Approach

1.1 Introduction

In W. S. Gilbert's "The Pirates of Penzance" appears the couplet:

"I'm very well acquainted too with matters mathematical,
I understand equations both the simple and quadratical."

It is a widely held belief that operational research is an abstruse branch of higher mathematics and that only wranglers can hope to appreciate it. Nevertheless, although it is perfectly true that mathematics enters into operational research, many scientists brought up through biology, psychology, economics or other subjects have been able to make very worthwhile contributions to both the development and application of operational research. To understand why this is so, it is necessary to trace briefly the development of the subject.

Until the second half of the last century, most industrial and business organizations were small, employing only a handful of people. The enterprises were usually owned and managed by the same individual. When expansion took place, it was no longer possible for one man to perform all the necessary managerial functions. Consequently, new functions grew up, such as Production Controller, Personnel Manager, Sales Manager, and so on. Each of these functions evolved its own particular sphere and mode of operation and competence.

Following the decentralization of the separate functions, it slowly came to be realized that many problems could not be isolated into the individual compartments that were being set up in large organizations. Although scientific developments were coming to the aid of the individual specialities created by this fragmentation, they were not coming to the aid of the overall executive function being created within the organization as a whole. As a result, it ultimately became imperative to have some method within the organization for coping with problems which spanned the various compartments. This led to the development of the ideas, if not the name, of operational research. For quite a long time, however, this kind of thinking

1

was applied only in a limited number of situations where it had become crystal clear both that a problem existed and that it did not naturally fall within the competence of any single department. Work carried out during the Second World War demonstrated that the range and number of problems to which this kind of thinking could be applied was much larger than previously visualized. The lessons learnt during this time were subsequently taken back, mainly through the redeployment of the personnel concerned, to various civilian industries and businesses.

The Council of the United Kingdom Operational Research Society, founded in the early 1950s, defines operational research as "the attack of modern science on complex problems arising in the direction and management of large systems of men, machines, materials, and money in industry, business, government, and defence." The Council goes on to state that "the distinctive approach is to develop a scientific model of the system, incorporating measurement of factors such as chance and risk, in order to predict and compare the outcomes of alternative decisions, strategies, and controls. The purpose is to help management to determine its policy and actions scientifically." Summarizing this definition it could be said that operational research is concerned with allocation and planning in complex situations involving scarce or limited resources. To put it in this way immediately highlights the close affinity which must exist between the operational research worker and those in other branches of management specialities, such as the accountant. The goals are common and, whilst the tools they bring to the job may differ, they are often complementary.

1.2 The Complexity of Problems

To illustrate the notions of conflict and complexity, consider the extremely common inventory (or stock control) problem. In a large organization, the formulation of the optimum policy to follow with regard to inventory will take into account certain elements of conflict. The Production Department will argue for a large inventory spread over few products. By this means they can have long runs on their machinery and thus produce efficiently. The Marketing Department will tend to urge a large inventory spread over a wide range of products. By this means they can meet the demands and requirements of any customer at a moment's notice. The Personnel Department will want to produce inventory in slack periods, on the grounds that there is a need to keep up morale and retain the skilled workers who, if dismissed, would be difficult to replace when demand rose again. The Finance Department will want to reduce the capital that is tied up in stocks and hence will tend to press for small inventories. It is noteworthy that this department generally seems to press hardest for reductions in stocks when times are bad, and allows the stocks to rise when times are good without undue comment. This tends to aggravate the operations of the firm when it is at a difficult period. Hence, even in this apparently simple problem, opposing views are likely to be put forward by different departments, and some basis of resolution is needed to decide upon the optimum policy that the firm should follow.

Most of the complex problems that arise in a business tend to be solved either by using past experience as a guide, or by applying rules of thumb that have grown up over the years. Whilst many of these rules work quite well in simple situations, they tend to break down as an organization gets larger or more complex. For example, consider the following simple transportation problem.

A firm has three factories located at Watford, Maidstone, and Manchester respectively. These factories have available 140 units, 120 units, and 50 units respectively of some product. Delivery of these units is required to three depots, 60 units to Birmingham, 100 units to Sheffield, and 150 units to London. The cost of moving one unit from any one factory to any other depot is shown (in shillings) in the main body of Table 1.1.

TABLE 1.1

Costs (shillings) per Unit Moved from Factory to Depot

Depots	Watford	Factories Maidstone	Manchester	Requirements
Birmingham	9	12	6	60
Sheffield	6	$13\frac{1}{2}$	$4\frac{1}{2}$	100
London	$1\frac{1}{2}$	3	9	150
Supplies	140	120	50	310

For example, the cost of moving one unit from the factory at Manchester to the depot at Birmingham is 6 shillings. If 5 units are moved the cost will be 30 shillings. If a transport clerk were now faced with the problem of scheduling these deliveries, he might approach it by looking at the table and selecting first the route that had the least cost. In this case it is the Watford–London route. He would then place as many units as possible on that route. In this case, 140 units would be the maximum, as Watford has only 140 units available for supply. Having done that, he would then select the next cheapest route, which is Maidstone–London, and place as many units as he could on that route. Because the London depot requires only a total of 150 units and 140 have already been supplied by Watford, the maximum he could place is 10. Having done that, he would then pick the next cheapest route, which is Manchester to Sheffield, and place as many as possible upon this route. This would be 50 units, as the Manchester factory only has 50 units available. Proceeding in this way, he would eventually arrive at the distribution pattern shown in Table 1.2, giving a total transport cost of 1,860.

TABLE 1.2

Transport Allocations

Depots	Watford	Factories Maidstone	Manchester	Requirements
Birmingham	— (10)	60	— (50)	60
Sheffield	— (100)	50	50	100
London	140 (30)	10 (120)	—	150
Supplies	140	120	50	310

(The figures in brackets relate to the optimum allocation.)

Now this is a perfectly logical and straightforward way of proceeding to carry out the allocation. A short study of the table, however, will convince the reader that this is not the optimum method of allocation. Indeed the optimum, which is shown in brackets in the table, gives an overall cost of 1,395; this is a very considerable reduction of some 25% in cost on the first attempt. Now although the clerk might, after a fair amount of effort, have reached this optimum solution by juggling around with the various quantities, it is unlikely that he would always reach the optimum before abandoning his efforts. Indeed, if the numbers of factories and depots were very much larger than given here, it is virtually certain that he would never reach the optimum by such methods. Hence, the rule-of-thumb approach used earlier is likely to break down when the situation is at all complex.

A second example (based on an illustration due to G. Coaker) points out the further necessity of defining precisely the characteristics which it is desired to optimize. A wood-working business, owned by Mr. Harvey, works an eight-hour day manufacturing and selling armchairs (A) at £3, bookshelves (B) at £2, coatstands (C) at £2 each. The business has three processes (P, Q, R) available which can be used only one at a time. The appropriate outputs are shown in Table 1.3.

TABLE 1.3
Wood-working Business

Process	Selling price	Process output (per hour)			Daily demand
		P	Q	R	
Armchairs (A)	£3	1	2	1	9
Bookshelves (B)	£2	2	—	1	11
Coatstands (C)	£2	—	3	2	9
Process cost per hour		£5	£6	£7	

Thus process P costs £5 per hour and manufactures one A and two B units per hour. The local retailers can sell up to a maximum of 9 A units, 11 B units, and 9 C units in one day, if such units can be supplied by the factory. The problem to be answered is how Mr. Harvey should best arrange his operations. If he aims to satisfy the market completely, it will be found that he can use process P for four hours, process Q for one hour, and process R for three hours, and thereby manufacture exactly the amounts demanded of each of the three products. His costs will then total £47, and his sales will realize £67, giving a profit of £20. If, however, he approaches the allocation problem by aiming to maximize his profit within the constraints of demand on each product, he will get a different answer. In fact, using process P and process Q for three hours each, his total costs will be £33 and his sales will be £57, giving him the maximum possible profit of £24. It should be noted that he will then make 9 A units, 6 B units, and 9 C units, so that he will not satisfy all the demand for B units. But he will have maximized his profit at the expense of not satisfying all the demand or working the plant fully.

These examples serve to show that simple rules of thumb may not be wholly adequate in the complex situations that arise in practice. Furthermore, it is necessary to define both the problem and its measure of performance rather more carefully than may have been done in many cases in the past.

1.3 Essential Characteristics

The first characteristic of operational research is that it attempts to deal with problems that arise in the operating of systems. The activity of any one part of an organization generally has some effect on the activities of other parts. Hence, to evaluate any decision or action within an organization, it is necessary to identify all the significant interactions and to evaluate their combined impact on the performance of the organization as a whole, not merely on the part originally involved. This orientation is contrary to the natural inclination of many researchers who try to cut the problem down to size and to isolate it as far as possible from its immediate environment. Many aspects of a problem are commonly eliminated in this way, reducing it to one that can then be handled by standard techniques or by judgment based on experience. Operational research, on the other hand, has a systems orientation and moves in the opposite direction by deliberately expanding and complicating the statement of a problem until all the significantly interacting components are contained within it. Put another way, this approach aims to investigate, over the entire area under the manager's control, the implications of the proposed solution to a problem. Such an enquiry should go to the full limits of the manager's responsibility, not neglecting the effects of policies made outside his area on the activity within his area. If this is not done, solutions can sometimes give misleading results. For example, an airline was concerned with the low average rate of utilization of its stewardesses on flying duty (expressed as flying hours per month) and wished to design a new method of scheduling their duties so as to raise this rate of utilization. A possible method of achieving this was found, in a manner which would not have a major effect on the morale of the staff concerned. Only at this point in the study did it become apparent that, because of the terms of duty defined for pilots and other air crew, the proposed schedules would tend to mean a lowering of their average flying hours. Hence the fact that the problems were so much interrelated meant that one should not consider them in isolation, since the optimum solution found for one problem might not be the optimum for the organization as a whole.

Secondly, operational research tends to use the team approach, welding together effectively personnel who have been brought up in a variety of different disciplines. Specialization in sciences became inevitable when the rate of increase of knowledge started to grow so enormously in the last century or so. Such subdivisions are, of course, artificial and not a natural phenomenon. Today more and more subdivision has gone on until the point has been reached where many pressing problems can no longer be treated fruitfully by an individual specialist. Hence, investigation by inter-disciplinary teams has become the only feasible alternative in many areas, although not all members of the team will play an equal part in an investigation. Furthermore, in the early years of development of operational research during the Second World War, there was a great shortage of all kinds of scientists. Consequently, when it was seen that operational research could make a significant contribution to military activities, staff had to be acquired quickly without being able to define very precisely the job specifications, and mixed disciplinary teams were formed out of sheer necessity. Out of this experience, however, came a recognition that the mixed team as such was valuable, and necessity had become a virtue. For example, an electronics engineer examining the problem of production and inventory control for a particular product may quickly perceive that fluctuations of inventory are a function of the length of time that elapses between changes in the market demand for the product and adjustments of the production level. The problem, to him, is one of designing a servocontrol system in which the relevant information concerning changes in the market demand is fed back quickly and accurately to the production control centre. At this centre, adjustments in production can be made in such a way as to minimize the appropriate cost function. He has, in fact, translated the problem into one of servo-theory which he knows how to solve. On the other hand, a chemical engineer may look at the same problem and formulate it in terms of flow theory and, having done this, he then has his own methods available for solving it. Which of the alternative methods of approach is the most fruitful depends on the circumstances. The project team must examine the alternatives and select an appropriate approach, possibly borrowing ideas from several different background disciplines.

The third essential characteristic is that of the adaptation of scientific method and the use of models. In research and development, experimental methods are used which are primarily based on the laboratory and pilot-plant scales of operation. With operational research this is not appropriate, in that the experimentation would have to be carried out by making trial changes within an organization which might, not unnaturally, be unwilling to allow such experimentation. There is, however, an alternative approach which is akin to the manner in which the astronomer works. He builds representations of the universe, or part of the universe, and checks whether the model that he builds fits the facts as he knows and can observe them. If it does, he then uses the model to predict future characteristics such as the eclipses of the sun or the states of the tide. When these models were first formulated by early astronomers they were not always very exact, but they were quite good for practical purposes. As time has gone on, the models have been refined and improved so that, whilst even today it is impossible to say that the models themselves are exact, they are nevertheless good enough for virtually all practical purposes. This is what the operational research man can also do. He tries to build a suitable model to describe the operations of the system which he is considering. This model will be formulated in terms of a number of variables, of which some are under the manager's control and can be altered precisely as required, whilst others are not completely under his control. Provided such a model can be found and formulated, then it should be possible to devise methods to use them in a predictive manner.

1.4 Types of Model

There are two basic types of model that the operational research worker commonly concerns himself with (although some other less common types exist which will not be discussed here). The first is the *symbolic* type of model where mathematical representations are made to describe the system concerned. As an illustration, some equipment-replacement problems fall into this category, a model being set up in terms of the cost of purchase of a piece of equipment, the costs of maintenance over time, and the resale value. Thus, if C represents the cost of purchase of a new item of equipment, m_i represents the cost of maintenance in the ith year, and S_n represents the resale value at the end of n years, then the cost of purchasing the equipment, using it for n years and selling it again is

$$\left[C + \sum_{i=1}^{n} m_i \right] - S_n$$

where $\sum_{i=1}^{n} m_i$ is a symbolic representation to denote the sum of the values of m_i from $i = 1$ up to $i = n$, i.e. $m_1 + m_2 + m_3 + \ldots . m_n$, i.e. n values in all. If, now, an infinitely long period is considered, the average cost per year, assuming replacement every n years over the time concerned, will be

$$\frac{1}{n} \left[C + \sum_{i=1}^{n} m_i - S_n \right]$$

The interval between replacements, n, would then be chosen such that this average cost is a minimum. Such a model is extremely simple as it stands, and therefore not entirely realistic. More complex variations can be introduced to remedy this defect. For example, it could be adjusted to include an allowance for any efficiency drop in the equipment which may occur over time. It could again be adjusted to take into account the taxation allowances obtainable on new plant; and the various cash receipts and expenditures can be discounted so as to allow for the precise points of time at which they occur and the rate of interest that has to be paid on capital outstanding. Perhaps, when these extra complexities have been introduced into the model, it may not then be capable of neat and explicit solution by standard mathematical techniques. Mathematical models of this type could then be explored numerically or graphically by substituting various values for the variables concerned, and getting a global view as to the way the effectiveness of the system changes with variations in the variables. Indeed, the ability to display many symbolic representations in either numerical or graphical forms provides a powerful approach to problem-solving in its own right, a point that is stressed on many occasions later in this book.

The increasing availability of high-speed electronic computers has considerably helped the development of symbolic models. It should be noted, however, that the virtue of electronic computers rests basically on their speed of operation. Many calculations that would previously have been possible, but wholly impracticable, by manual means thus become quite feasible. Computers can only carry out calculations for which the sequence of steps to be followed is well defined.

Of course, the size and complexity of mathematical models may be extremely great. For example, a model used in the petroleum industry to describe the operations of an inventory system, including its buying and selling procedures, required several hundred equations in order to make it realistic enough to be capable of describing the operations concerned. A computer was then essential in the ensuing analysis. Broadly speaking, it is always possible in principle to formulate a model, provided that it is feasible to get the executives involved in the organization to state the principles on which they currently operate the system under study. The subsequent use of the model may be rather more difficult.

A second type of model is the so-called *analogue* model. Probably the most familiar form of analogue model is that of the slide rule, in which quantities are represented by distances which are proportional to their logarithms. This enables multiplications to be performed by additions and divisions by subtractions. The analogue principle can, however, be taken considerably further with, for example, electronic circuits being used to solve various equations. Thus, many simple forecasting equations used for stock control schemes can be solved by having an electronic circuit with the appropriate responses and delays built into it. By feeding in the basic data concerning, first, the estimate of the current demand, secondly, the demand which has actually occurred, and, thirdly, the constants of the forecasting equation being used, a new estimate of the forthcoming demand is obtained.

An interesting analogue model of a mechanical nature can be developed for deciding upon the optimum location of a factory to minimize transport costs. Figure 1.1 (of a simplified situation) shows five towns at which varying levels of demand for a product have to be met from a single factory. The factory is to be located at the point which makes the total transport cost of deliveries to the

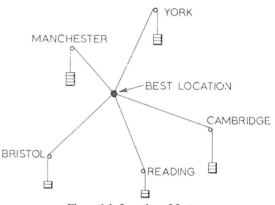

Figure 1.1   Location of factory

five locations a minimum. A vertically positioned map is drawn up, with the five locations placed on it, and friction-free pulley wheels put on the map at the five locations, with threads put over the wheels attached to weights which are proportional to the demand at the five points. These five threads are now joined to a single ring. The point at which the ring now settles, i.e. the point of balance of the various forces concerned, will be the point at which the total transport costs are a minimum. The truth of this can be demonstrated mathematically. One delightful feature of the model is that it is capable of very quick adjustments, without any need to solve complicated equations. For example, if a sixth location is to be introduced, this can be done immediately by putting in a further pulley wheel at the appropriate point and attaching a further thread with the new demand as the weight at the end of the thread. Alternatively, if the cost of moving a unit is twice as high on one route as it is on the others, this can be allowed for by making the weight at the end of that particular thread double what it would otherwise have been.

One important factor to bear in mind in the design of any model is that the number of variables that are incorporated considerably affects the amount of work involved. The labour of solving problems increases as the square, or even the cube, of the number of variables and whilst it is important to include enough variables for adequate realism, it is also important to begin with as few variables as seem likely to yield a useful representation. To this end, variables are often combined and it is important to be able to estimate approximately any errors which this form of condensation will incur.

1.5 The Phases of the Study

Any operational research project can be broadly split into six phases. These are

(a) Definition of problem and objective,
(b) Representation (or model) of situation,
(c) Test of model against actual conditions,
(d) Analysis of model to select optimum conditions to meet objective,
(e) Pilot implementation test,
(f) Implementation.

A few words will now be said on each of these phases in turn. First, the definition of the problem. This sounds easy, but it is often fraught with more difficulty than is apparent at a quick glance. Many of these difficulties stem from the necessity to decide how the performance of some system is to be measured. For example, a post office has frequent queues at its counters and aims to improve the situation. How is the cost of extra counter clerks to be balanced against the improved service to be offered to the public? In addition, some of the variables concerned are controllable, whilst others are apparently uncontrollable. The service times found at the post office counters are, to some extent, controllable, whilst the arrival intervals between customers are virtually uncontrollable. Hence, in setting down the problem, the yardstick by which various alternative solutions are to be compared must be defined and, if necessary, a method devised for combining the elements within the system so as to be able to achieve an overall measure of the effectiveness of each proposed solution.

In the second phase, some model or representation of the system has to be built along the lines already discussed. The complexity of this representation will vary enormously from problem to problem and, whilst complexity is not in itself of any merit, it is essential to have sufficient complexity for realistic results to be achieved. Once the model has been formulated, the third phase, namely its manipulation, is reached. Basically, the model can be manipulated in one of three ways. First of all, it can be examined mathematically by solving the equations concerned in a precise and exact way. Secondly, if the equations defy any unique form of solution, it can be examined arithmetically by a system of trial and error. Thirdly, even when it is not possible to put the mathematics in a formal manner, the model can be tackled by simulation techniques, an example of which is described below.

Whichever of these basic procedures is used to examine the model, it is equivalent to applying a form of search procedure which will provide a lead to the fourth phase of the study, namely the selection of the optimum set of conditions. In carrying out this phase, it is important not only to estimate the required set of optimum conditions under the various constraints built into the model, but also to examine how sensitive this solution is to changes in these constraints. Such manipulation makes it possible to see how critically the unique solution that was originally obtained depends upon the original assumptions built into the problem. This, in turn, can be of extreme importance in helping the manager to select precisely the set of conditions under which he is going to operate. If the solution is insensitive to changes in the constraints, he has considerably more flexibility than in a situation where the optimum is poised, so to speak, on a knife-edge.

The two final phases of the study are connected with its implementation, first a pilot implementation test, and then the full-scale implementation. Any proposed solution should be tested as stringently as possible before it is completely accepted and put into use. Neglect to do this can lead to vital factors being overlooked whose inclusion would markedly alter the solution. Experience suggests that the best form of pilot implementation is one where the solution is completely implemented for a portion only of the total system. Giving the proposed solution responsibility for running a complete, although small, section of the operations seems to provide a rather better form of discipline than trying to run the complete solution in parallel with the previous method of operation. Parallel running in practice seems generally to drag on interminably whilst a vast number of doubts are ironed out, with the result that there is no real clear-cut moment when it becomes advisable to cut off the old method and move over to the new. It is also important that, when the final implementation stage is reached, those responsible for the project should still be available. Only by being present then can they see that the solution is being correctly implemented and also that, if there are any snags, these are ironed out and the experience gained used in tackling any future problems of this kind.

1.6 Shipping Channel Illustration

The phases of an operational research study can be illustrated through a problem which arose with a steel works that was accepting ore from ships arriving from a variety of sources. The basic problem (due to D. T. Steer and A. C. C. Page, see reference 3 at end of chapter) is illustrated by Figure 1.2. Ships arrive in the bay outside the port which serves the steel works. They then have to pass through an entrance channel some thousand yards long, which they

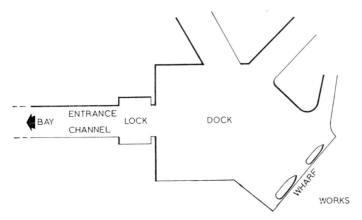

Figure 1.2 Layout of harbour and docks

can do for only an hour or two around high tide. Furthermore, if the ship is large, it may only be able to go through on certain high tides. Having gone through the entrance channel and lock, it is then moored in the dock area until one of the two berths at the wharf is free, when the ship can go forward for unloading. When the ship has been unloaded it waits in the dock until the next high tide and then passes through the entrance channel back into the bay. Any ship can normally pass through the entrance channel on the way out at the first high tide, irrespective of its size.

Clearly, the actual depth of the entrance channel affects the delays to the ships and their turn-round, in that a deep channel is open to use more frequently than a shallow one. The steel company has some interest in this delay, since they are paid a dispatch bonus which is linked to the turn-round time of ships, measured from their arrival outside the port to their departure from the entrance channel. Furthermore, although the steel company does not own the entrance channel they could pay to have it dredged to a greater depth than it is at present. The problem was to decide whether it would be worthwhile paying to have the entrance channel dredged and, if so, the amount of dredging which should be done. This forms the first phase.

The next phase was to set up a suitable model to describe the situation. It could not be a simple mathematical type of model, because the pattern of intervals between the arrivals of ships, both in terms of time and of the size of ship and type of ore it is carrying,

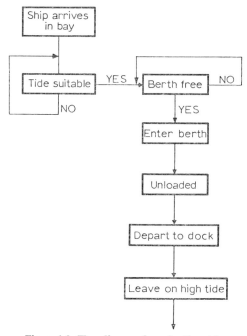

Figure 1.3 Flow diagram for unloading ships

could not be described in simple mathematical terms. What was possible, however, was to set up a flow diagram, such as Figure 1.3, which describes the sequence of decisions that have to be made after each ship arrives. Thus, a ship arrives in the bay; it waits there until the next high tide; if that high tide is suitable it goes through the entrance channel into the dock; if it is unsuitable it waits until the next high tide when it tries to enter the dock again. This procedure is repeated until the ship arrives in the dock. It will then, subject to any special rules laid down for the presence or absence of queue jumping, go into one of the two berths as soon as one or other is free. The unloading time is defined according to the nature and size of the ship and the type of ore that it is carrying.

When that time has elapsed, the ship returns to the dock and then moves out into the bay on the next high tide.

With a table giving the pattern of arrivals of the ships, a corresponding table of the tides and their height and a table of unloading rates, it is possible to simulate what will happen to the whole unloading system for different depths of entrance channel. From these results the corresponding level of dispatch bonus can be estimated. This forms the third phase of the study, namely the simulation analysis of the model. The fourth phase would put together the dispatch bonuses arising from having different depths of channel, against the cost of converting the channel to these different depths. When these two elements of cost and benefit have been combined, there will be some depth (it may, of course, be the present depth) which is an optimum. Before fully implementing this solution it is necessary to make some check on the results. One obvious check in this case would be to notice whether the simulated bonus result for carrying out no extra dredging agrees with the dispatch bonuses that have been earned over the past year or so. If these turn out to be in agreement, it is reasonably certain that the method of calculation is basically sound. Once this has been established it is then possible to go to the final stage of implementing the result obtained.

1.7 Form and Content

A manager reading this chapter may well be asking how it is possible for a group of operational research specialists, however ingenious they may be, to come into an organization and learn enough about it to solve problems that have given the organization difficulty for many years. The managers already there have probably taken years to learn about the organization and still have not solved these problems. In effect, any manager feels that his problems are different from, and more difficult than, those confronting any other manager. Familiarity breeds complexity, and even if operational research can help others, he may argue "how can it possibly help me?"

The manager is correct in thinking that his problems are different from anybody else's, but he is wrong in thinking that they are different in every respect. There is a distinction to be drawn between the so-called form and content of problems. In algebra the equation

$$y = a + bx$$

is the standard notation for a straight-line relationship between two variables y and x, the letters a and b representing constants. This is an algebraic formula which can be used for a wide range of problems but has no real meaning until it is applied to a particular problem, when specific numbers are put in for the constants a and b. For example, if x represents the temperature on the Centigrade scale and y represents the corresponding temperature on the Fahrenheit scale, the equation

$$y = 32 + \tfrac{9}{5}x$$

which is a particular case of the previous equation, provides a means of converting temperature on one scale to the corresponding temperature on the other. The original form has now been given content and is applicable to the specific problem of temperature conversion.

Any attempt at classification of problem areas is fraught with difficulty. One approach is through a subdivision arranged according to whether or not any of the elements in the problem have a chance factor. If all the relevant facts are known, any decisions needed can be made with complete certainty as to their outcome. Choice of a wrong course of action can then only be because of a flaw in the logical processes of selection. Non-certainty is caused when the decision-maker does not have knowledge or control of all the relevant facts. Such problems are more difficult to handle. The classical form of linear programming problem (which will be described in Chapter 3), namely the allocation of effort between a number of competing sources, is deterministic (and hence certain) in that the data relating to sources and inputs are completely defined and the outcome of any given allocation can be precisely calculated. Any departure from such definiteness brings the problem into the area of non-certainty. This latter area can be further subdivided into two categories. The category labelled "risk" is concerned with events having some repetitive nature and whose probabilistic mechanisms are well-known and understood and can generally be computed. The distribution of the intervals between telephone calls or of the times between successive breakdowns of production machinery are cases in point. The other category, labelled "uncertainty," is the fuzzier area of non-certainty that arises when, for example, a new product is to be introduced and market forecasts made. This is not a repetitive but a once-and-for-all situation and requires rather different handling.

Table 1.4 shows these three subdivisions and some typical types of problem that fall into each subdivision. Many of these problems will be discussed in the chapters that follow. The book is planned so that three chapters now follow on the first subdivision. Chapters 2 and 3 are for all readers, but Chapter 4 may possibly be withheld until a second reading of the book, particularly for those with more limited mathematical equipment. Chapters 5 to 7 deal with problems falling in the second category of risk, whilst Chapter 8 deals with

TABLE 1.4

Classification of Problems

Certainty	Non-certainty	
	Risk	Uncertainty
(1)	(2)	(3)
Resource allocation Blending (of oils) Transportation Sequencing Critical path	Simulation Queueing Inventory Forecasting	Capital investment Bidding problems Market launching Search problems

some concepts and problems in the field of decision analysis under uncertainty. The final two chapters of the book discuss applications of operational research in various fields of business operations and the problems associated with both organizing operational research within a firm and implementing the results. The appendices provide additional material, the first for those who wish to further their knowledge of the mathematical approach to programming (particularly allied to Chapter 4), whilst the second appendix provides a useful basic background for the full understanding of Chapters 5 to 8 inclusive. Appropriate references will be found at the end of each chapter.

REFERENCES

(1) *A Manager's Guide to Operational Research* by P. Rivett and R. L. Ackoff (Wiley, 1963).
(2) *A Guide to Operational Research* by W. E. Duckworth (Methuen, 1962).
(3) Feasibility and financial studies of a port installation, by D. T. Steer and A. C. C. Page, *Operational Research Quarterly*, June 1961, Vol. 12, p. 145.

2 The Programming of Resources —Networks

2.1 Background

Network analysis (or critical path analysis as it is sometimes called) provides a comprehensive, practical system for planning and controlling many large projects in construction, manufacturing, research and development, and many other fields. Its primary aim is to programme and monitor the progress of a project so that the project is completed in the minimum time. In doing this it pinpoints the parts of the project which are "critical," i.e. those parts which, if delayed beyond the allotted time, would delay the completion of the project as a whole. It can also be used to assist in allocating resources such as labour and equipment and thus helps to make the total cost of the project a minimum by finding the optimum balance between the various costs and times involved. Basically the method is concerned with the deployment of available resources for the completion of a complex task.

The main financial incentives for using network analysis are to obtain reductions in

(*a*) Lost production time, where productive capacity has to be closed while the work is undertaken,

(*b*) Interest on capital involved, where delay means idle capital,

(*c*) Controllable expenditure on resources, where better planning can increase the utilization of resources that are primarily overheads.

The experience of a number of firms which have used network analysis has shown that on suitable jobs this method can reduce the completion time for a project by 10% or more, and can increase the utilization of resources by at least 5%. The time reduction generally provides the most worthwhile achievement from this technique, and can often be obtained by a relatively low expenditure of effort on the network analysis itself. The following examples illustrate the financial prizes at stake:

(*a*) Alterations made to a paper machine normally operated on a 24-hour continuous basis cause loss of useful production time.

If the recovery rate of overheads from operating the machine is £50 per hour, then every day saved on a major maintenance job yields an increased contribution to profits of £1,200.

(b) Alternatively, a new factory is being constructed which is expected to achieve an annual profit rate of £1 million once it is operational. For every month by which the construction period of the factory can be reduced, there is a potential gain of about £85,000; for every week a gain of £20,000.

(c) The effect of a saving in interest on capital can be illustrated through a major project involving the raising of £10 million capital. Annual interest charges at a rate of 6% would amount to £600,000 per annum, so that if better planning could lead to the delay of the expenditure of £1 million of capital for just one month, this alone would result in a saving of £5,000.

(d) The resources of a department, e.g. the production department or development department, are often under-utilized owing to the fluctuating work load, and at other times may have to be employed at overtime rates to meet peak demands. If the cost of such a department is, say, £300,000 per annum and the utilization can be increased by, say, 5%, this is equivalent to a saving of £15,000 per annum, or may alternatively lead to an increase in output of 5%.

The following are some published examples of actual benefits that have been achieved from the use of networks:

(a) The use of PERT version of network analysis is credited with reducing the time taken to implement the Polaris weapon system in the United States by over two years. (PERT stands for Project Evaluation and Review Technique and is broadly equivalent to network analysis.) The use of network analysis is believed to be a "must" now for suppliers working on large contracts for the U.S. Government Armed Forces.

(b) Du Pont, the U.S. chemical firm, have used a modified version of network analysis to plan a $10 million project, and credit it with saving $1 million.

(c) Shell's Petite-Couronne refinery is saving 16% in time and 27% in men and money on their maintenance programme.

(d) Mauchley Associates quote the case of a construction project where a 9-month job was reduced to 7½ months, a reduction of nearly 17%.

(e) Du Pont cite a further example in which the use of network analysis reduced the time for a routine maintenance job from 125 to 78 hours, a reduction of over 37%.

Apart from the directly measurable benefits, network analysis can yield other important but less easily measured benefits, e.g. the earlier introduction of a new product to the market, or an enhanced ability to deal with last-minute alterations to a programme in the best possible manner.

The sceptic will argue that there is nothing new in network analysis and that Mrs. Beaton's verbal (and indeed verbose) description of how to cook the Christmas dinner is nothing more nor less than a network approach to the need to have everything ready at 1 p.m. on the great feast day. This is perfectly true, but it remains a fact that once the number of individual activities within a project reaches double figures, most people find it difficult to visualize the project as a whole by conventional means. Network analysis uses a pictorial flow diagram form of approach and aims to squeeze the utmost out of situations where a small saving in time or resources may mean very big money indeed.

2.2 The Method

The network process consists of two stages as follows:

(*a*) *Preparing the network*, which entails

   (i) Defining the scope and purpose of the whole project.

  (ii) Identifying the individual tasks, or "activities" as they are usually called, which go to make up the project.

 (iii) Determining the logical relationships between "activities" and "events"—the latter represent the start or end of the individual activities—and constructing the appropriate network diagram.

 (iv) Determining, for each activity, the estimated duration, the number of men to be employed from each trade or skill, and any possible restrictions (such as a specially scheduled starting date for a particular activity).

(*b*) *Analysing the network and reporting results*, which entails

   (i) Analysing the network to find those jobs which are important in determining the completion time of the project and those which are not so critical.

  (ii) Compiling a variety of reports to summarize the results.

The first stage requires the knowledge and experience of the men responsible for planning the project. Even these preliminaries leading up to the construction of the network can reap considerable benefits: the manager is forced to think in detail about the project well in advance; he will observe the precise way in which the various activities interact or compete for scarce resources; and it is likely that he will be able to improve upon his original plans even before the network has been formally drawn and analysed.

2.3 Drawing the Network

Each task within the total project is called an ACTIVITY and is represented in the network diagram by an arrow with a circle at either end, as shown in Figure 2.1, the letter A denoting the particular activity concerned.

A circle represents the start or end of the activity and is termed

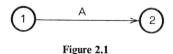

Figure 2.1

an EVENT, the number in the circle denoting the particular event. An activity can be identified by the pair of numbers belonging to the two events it links. In a typical project, some jobs must be completed before others can begin, whilst others can be carried

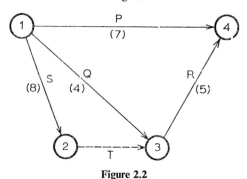

Figure 2.2

(Times in brackets are in minutes)

out concurrently. Consider, for example Figure 2.2 ignoring activity S for the moment. Activity P can be carried out at the same time as activities Q and R, but activity Q must be completed before activity R can commence. Suppose now that the further activity S is added. This activity can be performed at the same time as Q but must be completed before R begins. If this is shown as a single loop from event ① to event ③ this would be ambiguous as both Q

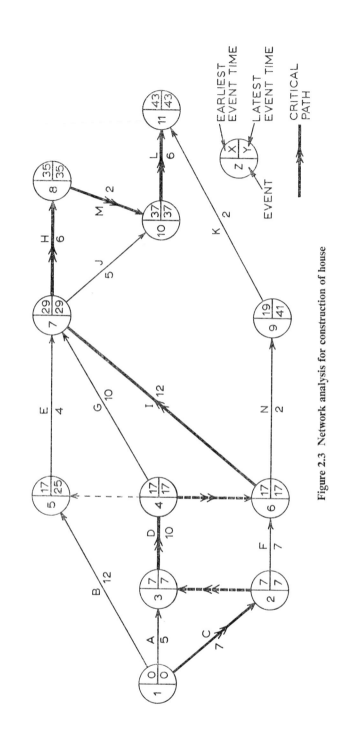

Figure 2.3 Network analysis for construction of house

and S would be identified by the same pair of events. Hence it is shown by the use of the DUMMY event T, as shown in Figure 2.2. Dummy activities have no duration and, apart from their value in resolving this type of logical difficulty, they have no other meaning. Note that in this particular example, activities Q and S could have been interchanged in position on the network without affecting the logic of the network as a whole.

It should also be noted that in a network diagram, arrows are used simply to show the relationship between activities; their lengths have no particular significance.

The minimum duration for the sequence of all four activities in Figure 2.2 is 13 minutes. This is because S must be completed before R is started, Q can be done while S is being completed, and P can be done while Q, R and S are being completed. Thus the path from ① to ④ via ② and ③ is that of minimum duration and is termed the CRITICAL PATH. Activities which appear on this path are referred to as CRITICAL, others as NONCRITICAL. Thus R and S are critical; P and Q are not. If either R or S is delayed, even by a second, then the whole project is delayed. On the other hand, activity Q could be delayed by as much as 4 minutes before becoming critical, i.e. before it would cause any delay to the completion of the project. The margin available for any activity before it becomes critical is referred to as its TOTAL FLOAT. The total float for activity Q is therefore 4 minutes, whilst the total float for critical activities is normally zero.

2.4 Illustration

Table 2.1 lists, in slightly simplified form, the activities and stages involved in the construction of a house. All the times shown are in units of "working days." No new activity can begin until the event logically preceding it (i.e. all the activities leading to that event's completion) has "occurred." The corresponding network is shown in Figure 2.3. Notice that a number of dummies have had to be included. Thus activity D cannot be started before both A and C are completed; activity E cannot be started before all the activities A to D inclusive are completed. The events are now numbered in such a manner that any event logically preceding another event has a lower number.

The longest time available for an activity is determined not merely by the time needed for its own completion, but also by the latest time by which it must be completed. Hence, although activity A (obtaining bricks) requires five days, to reach event number 3 needs seven days, because it depends upon the completion of activity C (preparing foundations). The spare time or float available for activity A is therefore at least two days.

The "earliest event time" of each event is the total activity time obtained by following the longest time path, where there is more than one possible path, to the event from the starting event (which is assumed to occur at zero time). Thus event ③ has an earliest event time of 7 because, although activity A requires only 5 days, activity C requires 7 and there is a dummy activity connecting events

TABLE 2.1

Activities and Stages in House Construction

Activity reference	Activity nature	Linking events	Estimated days for completion
A	Obtain bricks	1 and 3	5
B	Obtain roof-tiles	1 and 5	12
C	Prepare foundations	1 and 2	7
D	Erect shell	3 and 4	10
E	Construct roof	5 and 7	4
F	Lay drains	2 and 6	7
G	Wiring	4 and 7	10
H	Plastering	7 and 8	6
I	Plumbing	6 and 7	12
J	Flooring	7 and 10	5
K	Landscaping	9 and 11	2
L	Painting and cleaning	10 and 11	6
M	Doors and fitting	8 and 10	2
N	Lay pathways	6 and 9	2

② and ③. Event ④ then has an earliest event time of $7 + 10 = 17$. The remainder of the network can then be completed along similar lines.

Likewise, the "latest event time" for each event is established by working backwards from the final event. The earliest event time, 43, corresponding to event ⑪ is taken as being also the latest event time for that event. Event ⑩ will then have a latest event time of $43 - 6 = 37$; event ⑧ of $37 - 2 = 35$; and event ⑦ of 29 (the earlier of $35 - 6 = 29$ and $37 - 5 = 32$). This procedure is repeated until the starting event is reached where the latest event time will be found to be zero.

The longest time-path through the network, where any over-run would immediately affect the project completion date, is the critical path. This path will consist of all activities having zero "float," and these activities in turn can be identified as the activities leading to events where the

Float = (latest finishing time)
    minus (earliest starting time + time for activity)

is zero. In the example given, the critical path is formed by the sequence of events ①, ②, ③, ④, ⑥, ⑦, ⑧, ⑩ and ⑪. For a simple project such as this, calculation is straightforward and networks of up to 150 or 200 activities can generally be time-analysed manually. Larger networks are more economically analysed by computer.

2.5 The Analysis of the Network

Networks can be analysed from three closely connected aspects:

- (*a*) Time (i.e. to set work schedules and to find what leeway exists).
- (*b*) Resources (i.e. to formulate the distribution of trades, equipment, etc., required for the various activities).
- (*c*) Cost (i.e. to minimize the total cost of the project).

The result of such analyses is used as a basis for a plan of action, for example, to attempt to minimize cost for a given total time. These three aspects will now be considered in turn.

(*a*) *Time*
The aim of analysing a network from the point of view of time is to provide

- (i) The minimum time in which the project can be completed (based on the estimated times for the various activities); comparison of this with the target completion dates will indicate whether or not the latter can be met.
- (ii) A list of those activities which are critical, i.e. which must be completed on time if the target completion date is to be met. This focuses attention on those activities which need the closest control, since any reduction in the time taken will reduce the overall time for the project, while any over-run will delay the project. The critical activities are usually emphasized on the network by being shown in red or by a broad strip.
- (iii) A list of all other activities showing the amount of leeway (float) available, i.e. the amount by which their start or finish can be delayed without affecting the overall completion time.

This form of analysis provides a systematic procedure which identifies those jobs, often relatively few in number, whose improvement in terms of time will shorten the overall duration of the project. In many circumstances there will be possibilities of speeding up selected activities, usually by incurring extra costs. For example, the plumbing would normally be installed in the building in 12 days at a cost of £64 or in 10 days at £80 by working more overtime. Whether this is worthwhile or not will depend upon the value placed upon any time saved in the overall project. If plumbing is on the critical path and each day's saving in completion time for the whole project is worth more than £8, then such a change is worthwhile. If the saving is worth only £5 a day, then it is not worthwhile.

(b) Resources

The resources available, which are usually limited, may be required for a single project or for several projects running in parallel. The problem is to balance the requests for these resources so that the load on them is as even as possible and yet the projects are each completed in the shortest possible time. The advantage of using networks as the basis for the balancing the allocation of resources is that they show clearly which activities can be delayed, and by how much, without causing delays to the whole project. These considerations apply to labour (tradesmen, semiskilled and unskilled) as well as to various types of capital equipment (bulldozers, cranes, arc-welding equipment, etc.) which may be employed.

The procedure is to

(i) Analyse the requirements for each type of resource according to the various activities, project by project, period by period.

(ii) Analyse the total requirements for each particular resource, period by period, assuming that each activity is started at the earliest possible time.

(iii) Balance the resource requirements, where it is necessary, by delaying the least critical activities or by proposing a change in the resources available.

The balancing of resources in simple cases can be done by inspection of the tables resulting from these analyses and a re-arrangement of the schedules within the available leeway. For complex situations specialist help may be required in order to reach as satisfactory a solution as possible, without incurring excessive cost. Both the time and resource analyses may have to be re-worked after the total cost analysis has been made, as described in (c) below. This specialized procedure is sometimes referred to as RAMPS (resource allocation and multi-project scheduling). Computer programs are available to help, and one such program in general use handles up to six projects utilizing up to 60 resources and containing up to 700 activities. Broadly, by decreasing the input of resources, men, or machinery, there is an increase in their utilization but the project as a whole is delayed. Hence once again the problem of reconciling two conflicting objectives arises. The types of utilization costs that must be borne in mind are threefold. First, there are the premium costs that will be necessary to carry out the scheduled plan during periods when the normally available facilities are overloaded. Secondly, there are the costs of idle time when no work is available for men or machinery. Thirdly, there are the costs incurred on other projects when they have to wait for individuals or machines that are required on the priority project.

Whenever the availability of a resource is less than its maximum requirement in a network, some choice will have to be exercised in its allocation. Unless a random choice is made, some criterion is needed by which the most efficient allocation may be determined. The criterion used is the utilization as reflected in the float. By delaying a job with a large float, some of that float tends to be absorbed and the utilization of the resources consumed by that job is thereby enhanced.

(c) Cost
The object of analysing a network from a cost point of view is to minimize the total cost of the project, i.e. the sum of the direct and indirect costs. By "direct cost" is meant the cost of labour, material, etc., required to carry out the project. By "indirect cost" is meant the penalty for delaying the completion of the project, e.g. loss of profits.

The procedure is to

(i) Estimate the time taken by, and the cost of, the most critical activities if they were carried out normally, and the costs associated with each possible time reduction (e.g. by doing overtime) until the minimum possible time is reached.

(ii) Tabulate the direct costs for progressively shorter completion times for the whole project. These costs are calculated by reducing the time taken for those critical activities which cost least to reduce. Note that the critical path may change one or more times during this procedure.

(iii) Tabulate the indirect cost for each completion time, since it is likely to be affected by the time taken to complete the project.

(iv) Add the direct and indirect costs and hence locate the best time and cost combination.

Figure 2.4 shows graphically the result of carrying out such a procedure, the minimum cost being shown at point A.

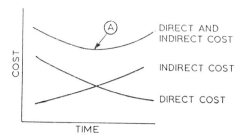

Figure 2.4 Cost versus time

2.6 Forming a New Organization

Although network analysis has largely been used on construction projects, it can be and has been used for administrative studies. For example, the technique was used by Whitehall (see reference (4) at end of chapter) in the planning and establishment of the Land Commission, one of the outcomes of the newly elected Labour Government of October 1964. After a few skeleton networks had been drawn up, the main control network, shown in Figure 2.5, was drawn. From this network a series of subnetworks was drawn up, each being used to control a particular area of activity. The principle followed was to have a hierarchy of networks which could enable a large number of activities—370 in this case—to be handled manually—a situation which would have needed a computer for regular evaluation if they had been combined in a single network.

The preparation of the main control network was divided into two stages:

(*a*) Determining the logical inter-relationship of the activities,
(*b*) Determining the time scale.

Under (*a*) there were five key events which shaped much of the logic. They were

(i) The publication of the White Paper (event ④),
(ii) The completion of the planning stage (event ⑳),
(iii) The completion of the buildings to house the staff (event ㉗),
(iv) The Royal Assent to the Bill (event ⑲),
(v) The appointed day when the Land Commission came into operation (event ㉘).

Certain special factors arose in the logic from problems regarding accommodation and the recruitment of senior staff.

Under (*b*) the activities were divided into those which could be regarded as forming the "shell" of the operation, over which little or no control regarding the durations could be exercised, and those where some flexibility existed, assuming that resources of manpower could be made available. The "shell" items were

   (i) the legislative activities,
  (ii) the accommodation activities,
 (iii) the training activities,
 (iv) the automatic data processing activities.

The remaining ("flexible") activities included

   (i) liaison with other bodies,
  (ii) systems design work,
 (iii) recruitment,
 (iv) trials.

This flexibility was exploited by planning staff recruitment so that the time required on each path was roughly equalized. This was a conscious departure from the usual practice of estimating the time required with given resources and possibly having a substantial float on some paths. It is good management practice that, on any administrative project, there should be the minimum of float and that all paths should be equally critical; this is also good for staff morale, as there is the implication that all concerned are being kept equally active.

2.7 Controlling the Project

A bar chart version of Figure 2.5, showing activities against a time scale, was used for day-to-day control of operations. The chart was kept up to date by weekly telephone messages. Formal progress reports were not needed and this system of communication proved easy, cheap, and effective. At the operational level, the various subnetworks listed in Table 2.2 were prepared and these networks were the responsibility of the individual officer in charge. Informal meetings, in the staff common room, on whose walls all networks were displayed, helped to ensure that sound communication existed between those responsible for the various subnetworks.

As always with a project of this complexity, activities did not run exactly as envisaged in the original network. Full advantage was taken of the flexibility of network analysis to investigate the effect of any delay and check the efficacy of any remedial action. It

TABLE 2.2

Subnetworks Prepared

Subnetwork	Date prepared (approx.)	Number of activities in subnetwork	Corresponding number of activities in main network
Automatic data processing	July 1965	74	7
Levy procedures	Oct. 1965	65	2
Staff recruitment	Jan. 1966	63	2
Training	Jan. 1966	141	9

proved necessary to undertake two major reviews of the project, the first in October 1965 when reasonably firm dates for all shell activities were available and again in April 1966 following the 1966 General Election. On both these occasions the main control network was redrawn and fresh time estimates prepared. The critical path for the project changed several times as networks were redrawn and activities under- or over-shot their time estimates. At one stage it ran through the items concerned with training and legislation whilst later still it was confined to the legislative items.

Overall the concept of the hierarchy of networks proved very effective and manageable by staff with little or no previous experience of network analysis. The concept induced a better sense of purpose in all concerned and enabled greater control over progress to be achieved than would otherwise have been possible.

There are many other administrative problems where networks may be of value. For example, the time taken to transport a pack of punched cards from one place to another is basically independent of the size of the pack, but the duration of a tabulation derived from such a pack of cards is approximately proportional to the number of these cards. The implication is that the critical path for the organization of the operations could change according to the amount of information being processed. In a punched-card installation with an increasing load, the point at which a particular machine within the installation would become critical could be calculated in advance by network analysis. Using such an approach can help to speed up the preparation of end-of-month accounts, statistical returns, etc. One recent British Prime Minister, Mr. Macmillan, has gone on record as stating that there are difficulties in attempting to control the economy using out-of-date statistics. In such areas the application of these ideas should give some assistance.

2.8 Fitting out a Hotel

A large modern hotel is a complex organization and the planning required to bring a new hotel into operation on a given date is a mammoth undertaking. In the particular case of a recently built London hotel, network analysis was used for this task and, as a result, it is believed that the time for the fitting-out stage was reduced from 12 months to 9 months. Figure 2.6 shows a particular portion, relating to one of the restaurants, of the overall network that was employed.

Once the network had been drawn up and analysed in the usual way, it was constantly updated at weekly intervals, using a computer. Each activity was the responsibility of one particular man, who might have dozens of activities under his control. There were about 3,500 activities in all. Unlike the previous problem, the activities handled by one man cut across the networks, e.g. one man might be responsible for carpets wherever they were to be fitted. Control was exercised through the weekly reports via the computer. The weekly print-out was arranged, not in the conventional order of activities or events in numerical order, but according to the managerial responsibility concerned.

Figure 2.7 shows a typical page of the print-out relating to one given week, some of the events concerned being shown on the network portion illustrated by Figure 2.6. An indication of how the situation is progressing is given on the right-hand side. All these events are due to start some time after the current review period. Nevertheless, the float figures show that, owing to other events being delayed, there are already some activities, indicated by negative float figures, which will be late. The critical path will, therefore, be prolonged unless savings can be made in some of the relevant durations estimated. For example, the delivery of menus and covers to the banquet area needs to be reduced by one week from 8 to 7 to avoid affecting the critical path.

This method of arrangement of a large project according to the responsibility involved is a very useful one for projects of this size. It enables individual managers to see precisely how the project is faring, how their own activities are affecting or are affected by other activities, and where bottlenecks either have occurred or may occur in the future.

2.9 The Cost of Using Network Analysis

The cost of using network analysis is made up of the costs of the time taken by

(*a*) the specialist,

(*b*) those persons providing the estimates of times, costs, resources, etc.,

(*c*) the cost of clerical assistance or of computer time if a computer is used.

These costs are clearly dependent on the project under consideration, and most of them are generally incurred once any planning at all is done; the use of network analysis, however, considerably reduces the time taken to revise any project plans compared with, for instance, revisions of bar or Gantt charts that are commonly used in project planning.

Since network analysis can commonly be expected to reduce the time taken for a project by at least 10%, and to improve the utilization of resources by at least 5%, it is possible to estimate the amount that can economically be spent on using it. For example, in a project estimated to take approximately ten months, for which the penalty for each month's delay in completion is £500, it would be economical to spend up to £500 on network analysis. Alternatively, if a saving on resources could be made through network analysis of £15,000 per annum, it would be worth spending up to that amount. However, it is unlikely that the use of network analysis would ever cost such a high proportion of the savings. If a large project with 1,000 activities were considered, the network might require

4 weeks' work by a specialist	say	£400
2 weeks' assistance from those concerned with the project	say	£120
Computer time or clerical cost	say	£100
		£620

This could then be justified for a job expected to take roughly ten months at a cost penalty of £620 or more per month, and few projects of 1,000 activities would be found in practice to have such a low penalty.

REFERENCES

(1) *An Introduction to Critical Path Analysis* by K. G. Lockyer (Pitman, 1966).
(2) *Network Analysis for Planning and Scheduling* by A. Battersby (Macmillan, 1967).
(3) *Industrial Scheduling* by J. F. Muth and G. L. Thompson (Prentice-Hall, 1967).
(4) *Network Analysis in Forming a New Organization* by W. S. Ryan (C.A.S. Occasional Papers, No. 3, H.M.S.O.).

3 The Programming of Resources— The Graphical Approach to Allocation

3.1 The Wood-working Business

In section 1.2 (page 5) the problem of Mr. Harvey's wood-working business was described. Basically his situation was that he had certain productive resources available and could make any or all of three products. The basic data are reproduced in Table 3.1.

TABLE 3.1
Wood-working Business

| Product | Selling price | Process output (per hour) | | | Daily demand |
		P	Q	R	
Armchairs (A)	£3	1	2	1	9
Bookshelves (B)	£2	2	—	1	11
Coatstands (C)	£2	—	3	2	9
Process cost per hour		£5	£6	£7	

As he only works an eight-hour day, there are limitations on the utilization of the productive resources which, together with marketing restrictions, form constraints to prevent Mr. Harvey from making as many as he might desire of each product. Assuming that his objective is to obtain maximum profit, one possible line of argument which Mr. Harvey might pursue runs as follows:

"Suppose that I use process R entirely by itself, as this is the one process that makes all three products. Then, using average outputs and costs, I can operate for only $4\frac{1}{2}$ hours per day and my output per day will be $4\frac{1}{2}$ units of A, $4\frac{1}{2}$ of B, and 9 of C. The total cost will be £31$\frac{1}{2}$ and the total sales revenue will be £40$\frac{1}{2}$, giving a profit of £9. I notice that this is well below the potential market for A and B and hence decide to "fill up" as far as possible

33

with process P which makes both A and B. Since process P produces 2 B type units per hour and the untapped market for type B is $(11 - 4\frac{1}{2})$, or $6\frac{1}{2}$ units per day, the maximum time I can take up on process P will be $3\frac{1}{4}$ hours per day. For simplicity, I decide to make my schedule 3 hours on process P, with $4\frac{1}{2}$ hours on process R. This will give total costs of £46$\frac{1}{2}$ per day and total sales revenue of £61$\frac{1}{2}$, leaving a profit of £15 per day. But this may not be the maximum, particularly as the market is not being completely utilized. I now notice that an hour on process Q produces £6 of profit, whilst on process R an hour produces only £2 of profit. Hence as much substitution from R to Q as is possible would seem desirable. In fact, only three hours of process Q are possible, as 9 C type units are the maximum that can be sold per day. The position now would be:

Production	P: 3 hours at £5	Q: 3 hours at £6	Total cost £33
Yield A	3	6	9 sales at £3 = £27
Yield B	6	—	6 sales at £2 = £12
Yield C	—	9	9 sales at £2 = £18

With a total cost of £33 and a total selling value of £57, a profit of £24 is left. Can I improve upon this result?"

Trial and error shows that this solution cannot be improved upon, but a trial and error procedure to ensure that this is so is tedious to say the least. Cannot, therefore, this type of problem be tackled in some more general way which guarantees obtaining an optimum production schedule?

3.2   The General Allocation Problem

Mr Harvey's wood-working business provides one illustration of an allocation problem. There are three main types of allocation problems.

(a) Assignment problems
In this group of problems, each of n units of one type has to be linked with one of n units of a second type in such a way that every unit has just one link. Each origin of the first type is to be associated with one and only one destination of the second type, and a table of effectiveness is available showing the cost, or profit, of making each possible link. It is wished to make the associations in such a way as to minimize (or maximize) the summed effectiveness. For

illustration, consider the following example, in which the tractors form the origins (!) and the various consumers' premises form the destinations.

A petrol company distributes petrol from its bulk storage depot to industrial consumers. For this purpose, it maintains a fleet of tractors and tank trailers. Since emptying a trailer at a consumer's premises usually takes about two hours, the tractor driver leaves the loaded trailer at the consumer's premises, picks up an empty trailer from either the same or another consumer, and returns it to the bulk storage depot for re-filling.

Assume that on a certain morning ten similar tractors have been sent out to deliver ten loaded trailers to consumers located in different parts of the city. After unhooking the trailers on consumers' unloading premises, the tractors are required to haul back ten empty trailers from the premises of ten other consumers. The problem is to assign these ten tractors to empty trailers in such a way that the cost of hauling back empty trailers is minimized.

The cost of taking back an empty trailer is known to depend on

(i) the total distance travelled by the tractor from the place where it was unloaded back to the bulk storage depot, and

(ii) the speed of travel.

Knowing these factors, one naive method of approaching this problem would be to determine the cost associated with every feasible assignment and then to pick the minimum cost assignment. Note, however, that the total number of feasible assignments is 3,628,800. Hence some quicker and more systematic method of approach seems necessary and efficient algebraic procedures and computer codes have been developed to achieve this result.

(b) Transportation problems

This class of problem is a generalization of the type described under (a) above. The table of effectiveness of the various possible linkages is no longer necessarily square: it defines the precise effectiveness when each of a number of origins is associated with each of a possibly different number of destinations. The total movement from each origin is known, together with the total movement to each destination. It is required to determine how the associations should be made subject to the limitation on totals. An illustration of such a problem, involving the transportation of goods from factories to warehouses, was described in section 1.2, and again efficient algebraic procedures and computer codes have been developed to solve the general problems of this type.

(c) Programming problems

In describing this group, the earlier groups of problems (*a*) and (*b*) are included as special cases. Since rather easier computational procedures are available for (*a*) and (*b*) these are used whenever possible. The general group involves a broad class of optimization problems dealing with the interaction of many variables subject to certain constraints.

For example, certain steel products may be obtained in a steel mill by using various combinations of raw material and hot-rolling, cold-rolling, annealing, normalizing and slitting operations. To be able to reach an optimal programming decision, all possible combinations of these operations and materials must be considered simultaneously. Here profit might be the objective to be optimized. Note, incidentally, that there is usually a big difference between programmes which maximize profits and those which minimize costs. Only if the product quantities are fixed or if the sales prices are directly proportional to the costs will the two programmes give the same allocation.

The constraints imposed on the process could include, for example:

   (i) Capacity limitations of each operational facility,
  (ii) Minimum amounts required for each product,
 (iii) Production requirements, quantity and/or quality,
 (iv) Delivery requirements,
  (v) Limitations on availability of operating fuels,
 (vi) Limitations on availability of raw materials.

To illustrate this general type of problem and the method by which its solution can be approached, an example will be described in some detail. The technique used for its solution provides a demonstration of the linear programming method. Such a method is applicable when the key elements are related directly (e.g. total variable costs are proportional to the volume of production). This property is called linearity and is referred to further in section 3.8. In this chapter a graphical approach to linear programming is described, whilst in the following chapter and in Appendix A a more mathematical approach is discussed.

3.3   The Transrad Company

A small company, the Transrad Company, assembles and markets two types of transistor radio, A and B. Currently 200 radios of each type are manufactured per week. It is clear to management that not all the facilities are being fully utilized and it is desired to formulate the production schedule that will maximize the profits. Some relevant facts concerning these radios are as follows:

Type	Total component cost per radio	Man-hours of assembly time per radio	Average man-minutes of inspection and correction time per radio	Selling price per radio
A	£10	12	10	£20
B	£8	6	35	£14

The disparity in inspection and correction time is due to the fact that some of the components in the B-radios are of cheaper and lower quality than those in A-radios. The company employs 100 assemblers, who are paid 10 shillings *per hour actually worked* and who will work up to a maximum of 48 hours per week. The amount of inspection and correction time used per week cannot be exactly forecast for any particular week, as long runs of successes or failures may occur. The inspectors, of whom there are currently four, have agreed to a plan whereby they average 40 hours of work per week each. However, the four inspectors have certain other administrative duties which have been found to take up an average of $8\frac{1}{3}$ hours per week between them. The inspectors are each paid a fixed wage of £40 per week.

Each radio, of either type, requires one speaker, the type being the same for each radio. Speakers are scarce, and the company can obtain a maximum supply of 600 in any one week. Their cost has been included in the components cost given for each radio in the table above. Only speakers actually used need be paid for. The only other costs incurred by the company are fixed overheads of £1,000 per week.

Under the present production schedule the company has a sales income of

$$200 \times 20 + 200 \times 14 = 6,800$$

(All monetary values from now on are expressed in £ unless otherwise stated and the £ sign will be omitted when there is no risk of ambiguity.)

The company's costs consist of

Components	$10 \times 200 + 8 \times 200$	$= 3,600$
Assemblers	$\frac{1}{2}(12 \times 200 + 6 \times 200)$	$= 1,800$
Inspection		160
Overheads		1,000

giving a total cost of 6,560 and a profit of 240. The company now has to ask itself whether this is the maximum profit which it can make. Clearly, any decision to change from the present manufacturing schedule must partially depend upon the marketing opportunities available. On being pressed, the sales manager believes he could sell up to 600 of either type, and 600 is clearly the maximum that could ever be sold because of the limitation on the availability of speakers.

To study the problem formally, let a represent the number of radios made of type A, and b represent the number made of type B. Then the cost statement given earlier can be re-stated formally as follows:

Sales income	$20a + 14b$	
Costs:		
Components		$10a + 8b$
Assemblers	$\frac{1}{2}(12a + 6b)=$	$6a + 3b$
Inspection		160
Overheads		1,000

Hence the profit is

$$(20a + 14b) - (10a + 8b) - (6a + 3b) - 160 - 1,000$$

or

$$4a + 3b - 1,160 \qquad\qquad\qquad\text{(i)}$$

It is important, however, to realize that a and b cannot be chosen at will. There are three constraints involved which affect the permissible range of a and b values. These constraints are derived from the availability of the speakers, the availability of labour for the assembly of the radios, and the limitation on inspection time.

Constraint	Resources	Amount needed (1)	Maximum amount available (2)	Form of constraint† (3)
I	Speakers	$a + b$	600	Col. (1) $\leqslant$ Col. (2)
II	Assembly	$12a + 6b$ (hours)	4,800 (hours)	Col. (1) $\leqslant$ Col. (2)
III	Inspection	$10a + 35b$ (minutes)	9,100* (minutes)	Col. (1) $\leqslant$ Col. (2)

* This figure represents the total available minutes less the time required for other duties (in minutes) or $4 \times 60 \times 40 - 500$.
† The symbol $\leqslant$ is shorthand for the phrase "is less than or equal to."

The values of a and b should now be chosen to maximize the profit function, at (i) above, subject to the three constraints given in the table. To illustrate this, Figure 3.1 shows the complete range of values of a and b that are permissible. The figure is in the form of a simple graph with a and b forming the two axes. Since a and b must both take positive (or zero) values, only the top right-hand part of the straightforward four-quadrant graph is permissible. But even within this quadrant not all values of a and b are allowable. Constraint (I) states that the sum of the values of a and b, or $a + b$,

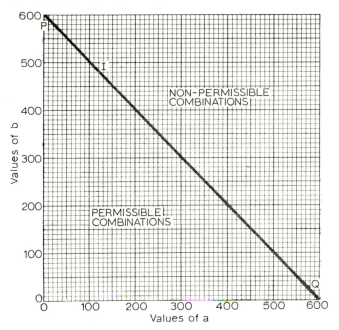

Figure 3.1 The constraint due to loudspeakers

must be less than or equal to 600. What combinations of values of a and b meet this restriction? Suppose that $a + b$ exactly equals 600. Then it will be found that this condition will be satisfied for all the values of a and b falling along the line marked I in Figure 3.1. Thus the points (400, 200) or (300, 300) or (0, 600) all satisfy the constraint exactly. Remember that in the shorthand notation (400, 200), the first figure 400 refers to the a or horizontal axis, whilst the second figure 200 refers to the b or vertical axis. For any point (i.e. combination of a and b) which falls to the south-west of line I the combined value of a and b will be less than 600, since the value of either a or of b, or of both, must be less than those for some point falling on the line I. Hence all points that fall in the area OPQ satisfy constraint (I). This already limits the possibilities, but further limitations must also be put down.

3.4   Additional Constraints

Not only are there constraints due to the availability of speakers, but also constraints due to the time required for assembly and inspection. These two forms of constraint can be dealt with in precisely

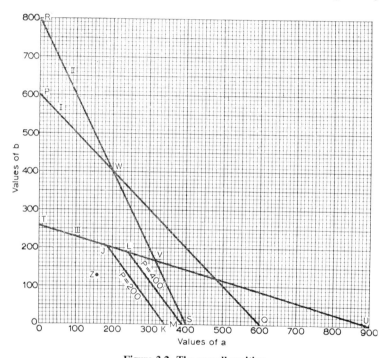

Figure 3.2 The overall position

the same way. For example, the constraint due to assemblers (II) can be expressed as

$$12a + 6b \leqslant 4{,}800$$

The line RS in Figure 3.2 shows the boundary between what is and is not permissible. Any combination of values of a and b to the north-east side of this line is inadmissible; any combination to the south-west is admissible. But the values of a and b must satisfy both the restrictions due to speakers and those due to assemblers.

Taking restrictions I and II together, the area for permissible combinations of *a* and *b* values is now OPWSO, a four-sided area.

The final constraint, that of inspection time, leads to the boundary line TU and the overall permissible area of combinations of *a* and *b*, taking into account all three constraints, becomes OTVSO.

It is now necessary to find the particular combination of *a* and *b* values within the area OTVSO which leads to the greatest profit. The profit function which is to be maximized is

$$4a + 3b - 1,160 \qquad\qquad \text{(from (i) above)}$$

Consider the pair of values of *a* and *b* corresponding to an arbitrarily chosen point Z inside the allowable area OTVSO. The profit corresponding to these values for *a* and *b* could be calculated from equation (i). Call this profit P_1. But as the point Z is *inside* the allowable area, it would be possible to increase P_1 by increasing the value of either *a* or *b* or both. Note that this is because the coefficients (multipliers) of both *a* and *b* in (i) are positive. The value of *a* or *b* or both can go on increasing until a boundary of the area OTVSO is reached. Hence the optimum location for Z to correspond to maximum profit must be on one of the boundaries of the permissible area OTVSO. Which boundary?

To determine this it would be possible to evaluate the profit for each *a* and *b* combination that falls on the boundary, but this could be rather time-consuming. A better way is to re-consider the profit function (i) itself, i.e.

$$P = 4a + 3b - 1,160$$

and note that for any fixed value of *P* the possible values of *a* and *b* giving rise to that profit *P* will fall on a straight line. Thus if *P* is equal to 200, any pair of values of *a* and *b* corresponding to a point lying on the line JK will give rise to a profit of exactly 200. If *P* is equal to 400, all the values of *a* and *b* corresponding to points lying on the line LM will give rise to such a profit. Note that these two "contour" lines of profit are parallel and, indeed, all the profit lines in this problem will be parallel to each other. What is now required is the contour line having the highest value of P that goes through some portion of the allowable area OTVSO. Inspection of Figure 3.2 suggests that the required contour line will be the one that goes through point V, since the contour lines have rising *P* values as they move over to the north-east corner of the permissible area. The values of *a* and *b* corresponding to point *V* can either be read off the diagram or, alternatively, obtained by solving algebraically

$12a + 6b = 4{,}800$

and $10a + 35b = 9{,}100$

as a pair of simultaneous equations. The solution is

$a = 315$ and $b = 170$

when the corresponding profit, P, from equation (i) is equal to 610. Hence the solution states that 315 radios of Type A and 170 radios of Type B should be manufactured to give a resultant profit of 610. This profit can be compared with the current weekly profit of 240.

3.5   Relaxation of Constraints

At the optimum point V, two constraints are being called into play, namely those of assembly and inspection time. The number of speakers is not a constraint in this situation, only 485 out of the available 600 being used up for the optimum schedule. This raises the question as to what would happen were it possible to relax those constraints which are critical to the solution, say by working over-time or by taking on extra staff. To answer this, a form of marginal analysis is carried out. Suppose that constraint II, relating the availability of assemblers, were made to read

$12a + 6b \leqslant 4{,}801$

in place of

$12a + 6b \leqslant 4{,}800$

This is recording formally that one extra hour of assembler's time can be permitted. The whole analysis outlined above could now be repeated and a new and modified solution found along the same lines as before. The revised solution is

$a = 315\tfrac{7}{32}$ $b = 169\tfrac{35}{36}$

and the new profit $P' = 610\tfrac{11}{36}$.

Ignore, for a moment, the fractional nature of the values of a and b and note that an increase of 1 hour in the amount of assembly time available has led to an increase in the total profit of 11/36. The method of calculation used has automatically included the £0·5 cost of an hour of assembler's time. Hence what this result is saying is that, at £0·5 per hour, an extra hour of assembler's time increases profit by £11/36. If it proved necessary to pay a premium rate of £1 per hour for such extra time, the change in profit would be

$\tfrac{11}{36} - (1 - 0{\cdot}5)$ or $-\tfrac{7}{36}$

converting a marginal profit into a marginal loss. Thus overtime at such a rate is not worthwhile. Note also that the revised production schedule, whilst increasing the number of A sets produced, decreases the number of B sets produced. Alternatively, consider the effect of changes in the amount of inspection time available. If the total number of inspection minutes available are raised by 1 (i.e. from 9,100 to 9,101), leaving the other constraints unaltered, then the revised solution is

$$a = 314\tfrac{59}{60} \qquad b = 170\tfrac{1}{30}$$

and the total profit is

$$P'' = 610\tfrac{1}{30}$$

Hence 1 extra minute of inspection time is worth 1/30, or 1 extra hour would be worth 60 × 1/30 or 2. Note that the profit evaluation used here considers inspection as a fixed cost in the total costs. Hence the cost of inspection time would have to be deducted from this apparent profit of 2 units. If such time could only be obtained at a rate of 2 per hour, then there would be no overall profit in obtaining the extra time. If it were to cost only 1·5 per hour, then there would be a further profit of 0·5 per hour obtained. Note also that, in this case, the revised production schedule calls for more B type sets, but fewer A type sets.

The summarized position, if marginally extra amounts of assembly or inspection time were available, is shown in Table 3.2.

TABLE 3.2

Marginal profit-changes

Extra hour of	Extra profit excluding cost of provision of manpower	Normal cost of 1 hour of manpower
Assembly time	0·81 (i.e. $\tfrac{11}{36} + \tfrac{18}{36}$)	0·50
Inspection time	2·00	1·06*

* This includes an allowance for "non-inspection" time in the inspectors' working week. If this is ignored the normal cost falls to 1·00.

Of course it would not actually be possible to operate extra single hours of either assembly or inspection time, owing to the fractional values for *a* and *b* that result. Nevertheless, these figures demonstrate the *rate* of improvement in profits achieved as the level of availability of time improves. Such rates must not, however, be extrapolated indefinitely. It would, for example, be quite wrong to assume from the marginal calculation that 100 extra hours of inspection time would automatically net precisely 200 extra profit, less the cost of the provision of the time. The amount may be affected by whether or not other constraints come into play. Hence for large changes it would be necessary to re-establish the profit actually achievable in the same way as before and the reader is invited to investigate the revised situation for himself. Like the correct use of marginal costing figures, these marginal profit figures are valuable in showing the trends.

3.6   A Minimum Cost Problem

The problem just discussed aimed to maximize profits. Linear programming can equally well be concerned with minimizing some function. For example, the quality of a product is specified by the number of units of a certain attribute Z contained in each ton. It is desired to make 1 ton of this product containing at least 50 units of Z at minimum cost. The raw materials shown in Table 3.3 are available—how much of each should be purchased?

TABLE 3.3

Ingredients and Costs

Material	Units of Z per ton of material	Cost per ton (£)
A	30	80
B	40	50
C	80	70
D	100	90

Here the total cost is to be minimized and the solution will consist of finding the cheapest mixture of the four materials which contains at least 50 units of Z per ton.

The problem can be solved graphically, through a slightly different approach to that used earlier. Figure 3.3 shows the cost per ton of each material and the units of Z per ton. Now any compound formed from A, B, C and D will have costs and Z-content represented by a point inside the area ABCD on Figure 3.3. For example, if a mixture is made consisting of A and C in a 50:50 ratio, then the characteristics of the mixture as to cost and Z-content will correspond to the point in Figure 3.3 which bisects the line joining A to C. Now MN divides the allowable mixtures, from a Z-content point of view, from the non-allowable mixtures. Only mixtures to the right of MN need be considered. As the cost is to be minimized, a mixture is

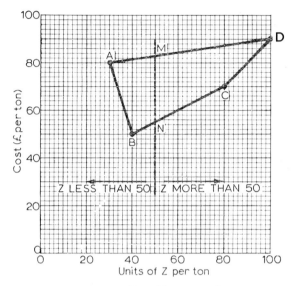

Figure 3.3 Allowable compounds

required which is as far down the graph as is possible. This is achieved at point N where the line MN crosses the line BC. At this point BN = ¼BC (found either by measurement on the graph or by simple algebra) and hence the mixture consists of 3 parts of B to one part of C. The cost, again read from the graph, is £55 per ton.

3.7 Power and Limitations

In general, the use of linear programming obtains a specific solution to a particular problem. Now, if a factory can manufacture 10 different products and only one constraint is placed on the manu-facturing schedule, say time, then the optimum production schedule will contain just one product. It would be the product whose profit per unit of production time is highest. If two constraints were placed on the system, say time and material availability, the opti-mum solution need only contain at most two products. As an illustration that this is so, suppose that the solution to a particular programming problem containing three products, A, B and C, appeared to suggest the schedule in Table 3.4.

TABLE 3.4

Trial Allocation

Product	Profit per unit time (£)	Constraints per unit time		Initial allocation
		Material used	Time used	
A	2	5	1	4
B	3	3	1	4
C	4	7	1	2
Total	—	46	10	Profit = 28

Then it would be possible to improve the proposed allocation, which gives a profit of £28, by transferring all the time spent on A to B, since that provides an increase in profit per unit time and a reduction in usage of material. The solution would now read:

B 8 hours,   C 2 hours,   Profit £32

and not all the material would be used, some 8 units being left over. A further improvement could be made by increasing the time spent on product C; each extra hour taken from product B would provide $4 - 3 = 1$ extra unit of profit but use up a further $7 - 3 = 4$ units of material. Hence only two hours can be so transferred, giving a final solution of

B 6 hours,   C 4 hours,   Profit £34

Note that two products appear in the solution (in some cases only one product may appear) but no higher profit solution exists with more than two products. In general, if there are n constraints (time, labour, raw materials, marketing, etc.), then only n or fewer products need appear in the final optimum solution.

Linear programming provides a technique which can achieve, in a systematic manner, the optimum choice from amongst a great number of alternative allocations. Thus, suppose a small firm is faced with the problem of selecting its product line from amongst ninety possible goods. Imagine that the firm has ten scarce resources or constraints on its programme of manufacture, so that it may be expected to produce ten items or less for the optimum situation. The number of theoretically feasible solutions to the problem can be shown from standard permutation and combination theory to be in excess of 17×10^{12}. Therefore, if a conscientious management were to devote even one second to the examination of each of these possible product-line combinations and were to spend 12 hours per day and 365 days per year on the task, the job would require over 1 million years to complete! What happens, of course, when such a decision has to be taken by traditional methods is that only a very small subset of the possible combinations is actually considered and, as a result, the likelihood that some of the best possibilities will be overlooked is very great indeed. Linear programming has to its credit a very noteworthy achievement in devising methods of solutions to such large problems so that, with the aid of computers, they can be solved in a matter of minutes or even seconds.

3.8 Linearity

Like all techniques, the results achieved depend to some extent upon the validity of the assumptions made, in particular the assumption of linearity, i.e. that the constraints can be expressed as simple linear or straight-line relationships between the variables. Although this may well be true for a certain range of problems, e.g. many transportation problems, this is not likely to be true for a wide range of economic problems. If one or more of the constraints can be represented only by a curved boundary, rather than by a straight line, the principle is still very similar to that shown earlier, although it may now be found that the optimum solution does not lie at a vertex of the allowable region, but on some edge of the curved part of its boundary round the allowable region. (Note that this is theoretically possible with a set of linear boundaries, but if this is so, then any point on the boundary concerned within the allowable region will give rise to the same optimum profit, i.e. there are an infinite number of optimum solutions, each giving rise to the same profit.) If, however, the profit function itself is non-linear, then, whether or not the constraints are linear, the optimum solution need not be at the edge of the allowable region, but could be in the interior.

Provided that the profit function can be formulated explicitly, this condition is easily detected by a sensitivity analysis. The problem is then usually dealt with by a related but more complicated technique known as separable programming or, more simply, by adding additional linear constraints. Recourse should be made to the specialist in such situations.

Sensitivity analysis of the kind described later in section 4.4 can be used to indicate how far the profit function can deviate from being linear and the linear programming solution still remain optimal. Troubles may be experienced if the extent of these non-linearities are difficult to estimate. In certain circumstances, even if the non-linearity is extremely slight, the error made by using linear programming can be substantial. W. J. Baumol, for instance (in reference 5 at the end of the chapter), has shown that the unmodified linear programming solution to a number of problems of a practical type can give poorer results than a more or less randomly selected initial allocation. This is not to say that linear programming is of no use, but merely to point out that it needs to be applied with care, and specialists should be consulted whenever doubt arises as to its applicability. In the following chapter some more complex problems in linear programming, where there are quite a large number of variables and constraints concerned, are discussed from the point of view of the user of the technique.

REFERENCES

(1) *Linear Programming and Extensions* by G. B. Dantzig (Princeton) (particularly Chapters 1 to 3).

(2) *Linear Programming, Methods and Applications* by S. I. Gass (McGraw-Hill, 1964).

(3) *Quantitative Approaches to Management* by R. I. Levin and C. A. Kirkpatrick (McGraw-Hill) (Chapter 8).

(4) *Linear Programming and the Theory of the Firm* by K. E. Boulding and W. A. Spivey (Macmillan) (Chapter 3).

(5) Errors produced by linearization in mathematical programming, by W. J. Baumol and R. C. Bushnell, *Econometrica*, Vol. 35, 1967, pp. 447–471.

4 The Programming of Resources— The Mathematical Approach to Allocation

4.1 The Approach

In the previous chapter the transistor radio problem was examined graphically to a large extent. This was possible because there were only two types of radio involved, A and B. If a third type, C, were added, this method would be impossible except by visualizing it in a three-dimensional geometrical form. If a fourth type, D, were added, the problem would become completely impossible in a geometrical idiom. Hence other approaches must be found. The most common approach is a mathematical procedure known as the simplex method. This is described in detail in Appendix A, and appropriate computer codes are widely available. It is not necessary to understand the appendix in order to follow the remainder of this chapter, although those readers possessing a knowledge of elementary algebra will obtain extra value from this chapter if they study the appendix at this stage. The remainder of this chapter will be concerned with the discussion of two examples. These will be discussed from three angles: first, the nature of the problem being tackled and its formulation in a linear programming context; secondly, the form in which solutions are obtainable from the simplex procedure; and thirdly, some of the practical implications inherent in the solution.

4.2 A Handling Equipment Problem

The first problem to be described is concerned with the feasibility of reconciling marketing policy with production restrictions in a firm which manufactured materials handling equipment. The firm found itself in a position where it seemed to be getting orders for "specials" without consequent orders for standard equipment. As a result, it was unable to take advantage of a flow-line type of production; it also gained the reputation for the manufacture and supply of specials, thus aggravating its existing problem. The firm decided that they must rationalize their products and product groupings. In doing this the firm was prepared to revise drastically their ideas as to which were the most profitable lines. It realized that it might then prove best to reduce the manufacture of certain products to a much lower level.

Talks with the management revealed that one of their basic concerns was with the amount of capital tied up in stocks. The large sum involved arose to a considerable extent because of the willingness to build specials which, in turn, required components of non-standard dimensions. The special components often had to be bought in from outside and, as a result, there were long lead times attached to these parts, causing the associated components to be held over this same long lead time. Even for certain standard items bought in from outside, the firm did not appear to be given the same attention as larger customers by the manufacturers of these components. It was felt that if the specials could be eliminated or reduced, then the overall stock-holding would be drastically cut. The problem thus resolved itself into determining which product groups were the most profitable to make and which groups could be dropped from production or run at a nominal level.

4.3   The Basic Data

The basic data are set out in tabular form in Table 4.1. The range of products manufactured was divided into eleven basic product groups. Information on the average number of hours taken for single units in each product group to pass through each of the five production departments was collected and analysed to give the figures in the left-hand portion of Table 4.1. The five production departments are shown as column headings and the eleven product groups are shown down the left-hand side. The total daily capacity of the five departments is given in the bottom row, two of the departments having so much capacity that they do not provide any constraints in practice. Other data, shown in the right-hand portion of the table, relate to the various costs, giving rise to an estimated profit margin for each product. In obtaining all this information, so effortlessly summarized and presented in Table 4.1, a great deal of work was necessary, and management was forced to focus their attention on a number of matters which had previously been neglected under the pressure of time. This in itself proved to be an extremely valuable part of the exercise.

The data are now in a form to which the linear programming approach may be applied. The problem is to find the mix of products which can be made so that the total margin achieved is a maximum,

TABLE 4.1
Basic Data

Product group	Actual hours required per item					Direct labour cost	Cost of material	Average selling price	Margin
	Fabricating	Machining	Assembling	Spraying	Inspecting and testing				
Transporting units	45·00	35·00	12·00	3·50	0·50	50	257	650	343
Conveying units	45·00	35·00	12·00	3·50	0·50	43	247	600	310
Lifting (N) units	50·00	30·00	14·00	4·50	0·50	57	417	1,100	616
Storing units	50·00	30·00	15·00	5·00	0·50	65	392	1,250	893
Loading units	50·00	100·00	22·00	6·00	0·75	116	625	1,828	1,087
Lifting (L) units	55·00	100·00	26·00	10·00	0·75	106	1,290	2,100	704
Lifting (M) units	50·00	100·00	15·00	10·00	0·75	94	858	1,900	948
Carrying units	175·00	100·00	75·00	15·00	3·00	211	3,522	5,100	1,367
Handling units	4·00	12·50	3·00	1·50	0·75	11	32	100	57
Hoisting (G) units	0·25	5·00	0·50	0·10	0·25	3	5	22	14
Hoisting (H) units	1·50	13·00	2·00	1·00	0·50	9	33	105	63
Approx. total daily capacity (standard hours)	438	1,043	633	—	—				

Note: Fabricating includes cutting, pressing and welding.
Margin = Selling price − (Direct labour + Materials).

while at the same time the constraints due to the capacities of the various departments are met. The information can be laid out in the form of a matrix array as described in Appendix A and analysed appropriately. After a number of trial solutions which are successively improved, a final and optimum solution is obtained. The form in which this appears is shown in Tables 4.2 and 4.3 and attention will now be concentrated on the information to be extracted from those tables.

4.4   The Solution and Its Interpretation

The optimum combination, indicated in Table 4.2, is to make 6·8 storing units and 64·5 hoisting (H) units per day. This corresponds

TABLE 4.2

Optimum Solution from Linear Programme

Product	*Output per day*
Storing units	6·8
Hoisting (H) units	64·5
All other units	nil
Total margin per day	£10,152
Spare capacity	*Hours per day*
Assembly shop	401·7
Fabricating	nil
Machining	nil

to 1,705 storing units and 16,125 hoisting (H) units per annum, and will give a total margin of £10,152 per day, or £2,538,000 per annum (which compares with an existing margin of approximately £1·3m per annum).

If this optimum combination is made, Table 4.2 also indicates that there would be 401·7 hours per day capacity still available in the assembly shop, but that the capacity of the other two departments with capacity constraints would be fully utilized. Note that the original conditions for this problem suggested three constraints, whilst the final solution contains just two products. This arises because the constraint of assembly time is dominated by the other two constraints.

The reason that the other product groups do not appear in the optimum solution is that the margin on them is not high enough to justify using the scarce resources, fabricating and machining, on them. Clearly if the margin on any one of these omitted products were steadily increased, there would come a point when it would be worthwhile to include this product in favour of one or other of the two products in the current solution without diminishing the overall margin achieved. The increase in margin which would be necessary to bring each of the product groups in turn into the optimum solution without diminishing the overall margin achievable can be obtained from the linear programming solution and is indicated in Table 4.3.

TABLE 4.3

Minimum Increase in Margin on Each Product Group to Make Production Worthwhile

Product group	*Minimum increase in margin necessary* (£)	*% increase on selling price*
Carrying units	1,744·0	34
Conveying units	517·5	86
Transporting units	484·5	75
Lifting (L) units	478·4	24
Lifting (N) units	277·0	25
Lifting (M) units	154·0	8
Handling units	44·1	44
Loading units	15·0	1
Hoisting (G) units	4·9	22

For example, if the margin on lifting (M) units were increased by 154 from 948 to 1,102, then it would be found that the optimum solution would just include some lifting (M) units and the total margin would still be at least £2,538,000 per annum. Any smaller increase than 154 would make it impossible to raise the total margin obtainable, whilst including some (M) units in the optimum solution. An alternative way of looking at the situation is to argue that each lifting (M) unit included in the production schedule at current prices loses a possible margin otherwise obtainable of 154. The list above gives the minimum margin increase per product group to ensure incorporation in the overall optimum solution. The final column of the table shows these increases expressed as a percentage of the existing selling prices. This is a form of sensitivity analysis.

The value of an additional productive hour in the departments fully used is also obtainable from the linear programming solution, as was done for the Transrad Company in Chapter 3. Thus the availability of an extra hour in the fabricating department would produce 16·1 extra margin (of course, the previously found production schedule would have to be revised to achieve this gain). The cost of providing this extra hour of capacity would also have to be borne in mind as, up to now, the costs of provision of the five departments have been treated as overhead (i.e. constant) items. Any additional cost would, therefore, have to be deducted from the profit of 16·1 apparently obtainable. An extra hour of machining time would similarly be worth 3·0.

4.5   Further Implications

The "robustness" of the optimum solution, in terms of the products which appear in it, may be critically dependent upon the accuracy of the margins imputed to each of the product groups. To test whether or not this is so, the margins were altered by 5%, in such a way that the margins on each of the two products currently appearing in the final solution were reduced by 5%, whilst the margins on each of the nine products not appearing in the current solution were increased by 5%. The linear programme was then reworked and the revised solution was found to be as follows, all quantities expressed per day:

	Revised solution	Original solution
	8·2 Loading units	6·8 Storing units
	16·7 Hoisting (H) units	64·5 Hoisting (H) units
Profit	£10,350	£10,152

Hence, although the total profit changes by very little, the optimum mix of product changes quite markedly. Such an alteration suggests that the cost data ought really to be accurate to something better than 5% in order to be entirely confident of the solution obtained.

The solution pursued so far in this analysis has treated as constraints only the capacity restrictions of the various production departments. It has been implicitly assumed that the firm could sell everything that it could produce. This initial linear programme solution gave the manager a clear view of the apparently ideal programme under such circumstances and, once that was known, he could redirect the firm's sales effort so as to sell more of the high profit items and so replan its production facilities to make its sales pattern as profitable as possible.

The next step was to introduce several marketing restrictions according to what it was believed could be sold. This would have the effect of limiting the production of individual products to specified quantities. After a full discussion with the managers concerned, limitations were placed on each product, due either to production considerations or to marketing restrictions, and whichever restriction was the harsher was the one incorporated in the final re-work. When these restrictions were incorporated—details are not given here—the optimum combination gave a margin of £7,780 per day and included a varying degree of production from eight of the eleven product groups. Further analysis would give the marketing department a choic of different price–quantity combinations to choose from.

Additional points which emerge from the solution are suggestions as to those areas where method study might ease the bottlenecks, i.e. in fabricating and machining, and where preventative maintenance may yield a high return.

4.6   A Problem in Paper-making

The second problem to be discussed concerns paper-making. Paper mills produce paper in reels of a given width, the width depending upon the particular paper machine concerned. Customers require reels of paper of varying widths (less than the machine width) and these are "fitted" together to come as near as possible to the width of the manufacturing machine. The machine reels are, therefore, cut to meet the customers' requirements, and there will usually be some waste at the edge of the reel in the form of an offcut which provides too small a width for any customer. The manufacturer aims to put the reel widths ordered from him together in such a way as to make the total edge (or trim) loss as small as possible. This "putting together" of ordered reels to fit the paper machine is commonly referred to as the deckling problem.

The basic deckling problem starts with a single paper machine of given width making one grade of paper only and a set of orders. These orders will normally be for reels of a standard length, but of varying widths, each width usually only a fraction of the width of the paper machine. It is then required to fit the orders together in such a way that the best possible use is made of the machine. For example, suppose the paper machine width is 90 in. and the only sizes of paper ordered are 21 and 13 in. wide respectively, for each of which a number of orders has been obtained. Then the possibilities as to ways in which orders of these widths can be put together are shown in Table 4.4.

Combination 3, for example, shows that two 21 in. reels can be combined with three 13 in. reels to be cut out of a complete 90 in. width to leave 9 in. of trim loss which will be wasted. In practice the trim loss paper is repulped, so that the material is not completely wasted, but the processing costs are lost. It is assumed that the weight of paper produced is proportional to its area, so that, for

TABLE 4.4

Permissible Combinations of Reels

Combination	Number of 21 *in.* reels	Number of 13 *in.* reels	Trim (deckle) loss (in.)
1	4	0	6
2	3	2	1
3	2	3	9
4	1	5	4
5	0	6	12

example, the production of 1 cwt. of 21 in. paper using combination 4 will lead to the simultaneous production of $5 \times \frac{13}{21}(=3\cdot1)$ cwt. of 13 in. paper and $\frac{4}{21}(=0\cdot19)$ cwt. of trim loss.

Now if the overall requirement is to make 40 cwt. of 21 in. paper and 70 cwt. of 13 in. paper, then linear programming shows that the best solution is

Combination 2   20·06 cwt. of 21 in. plus 8·28 cwt. of 13 in.

together with

Combination 4   19·94 cwt. of 21 in. plus 61·72 cwt. of 13 in.

giving a deckle loss of 3·80 cwt. of 3·3%. Note that there are two constraints in this problem, namely that the amount of 21 in. paper is at least 40 cwt. and the amount of 13 in. paper is at least 70 cwt. The solution, therefore, will only involve one or, at most, two of the five possible combinations.

As the number of order sizes increases, the magnitude of the programming problem grows disproportionately large and the difficulties of producing an optimum solution by inspection or by trial and error become very great. Similarly, if more than one paper machine is brought into the problem, possibly of different widths, the complexity is considerably increased. In such circumstances, the resulting linear programming problem can be solved only on an electronic computer using the appropriate program. Briefly, all feasible combinations are produced on the computer. From these, potentially useful solutions are extracted, bearing in mind the various machine restrictions, and eliminating those combinations which are inferior to simple mixtures of other combinations. An optimum solution, in which total deckle loss is a minimum, is then selected. This procedure tacitly assumes that deckle loss is the required quantity to minimize, which may well be so if there are no further processes through which the paper passes, although frequently delivery and storage problems have to be considered as well. But a new factor of a different kind enters if the paper also has to pass through further processes, such as a more expensive coating process. It may then be more profitable to use the coating capacity as efficiently as possible, even at the expense of increasing the trim loss on the paper machines making the base paper. The following study of

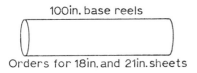

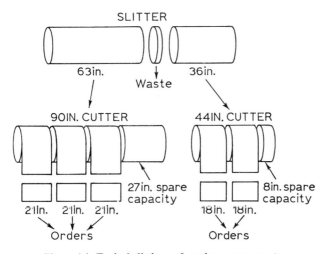

Figure 4.1 Typical slitting and cutting arrangements

such a situation is based on a paper written by E. Jowett and W. S. Harvey of Wiggins Teape Research and Development Ltd. (see reference 3 at end of chapter).

Figure 4.1 illustrates a typical situation where 100 in. base reels of paper are slit into two parts for cutting into sheet paper of 21 in. and 18 in. width, the lengths required being in the ratio of 3:2. Two cutters are available, one 90 in. wide and the other 44 in. wide. Trim waste on the reels of base paper is minimized by slitting and cutting as shown in the figure. If, however, the paper has to be coated before it is cut into sheets and the available coaters are also 90 in. and 44 in. wide, then the method of slitting and cutting shown in Figure 4.1 will waste coating capacity (27 in. on the 90 in. coater and 8 in. of the 44 in. coater). If the objective of the planning were to reduce the coating waste capacity to a minimum, in place of reducing the base paper trim loss to a minimum, the paper should

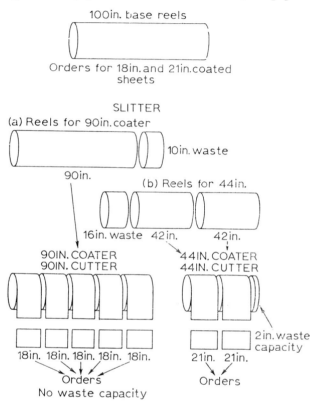

Figure 4.2 Reduction of coating waste

be slit and cut as shown in Figure 4.2. There is now, however, a much larger trim loss. Clearly there will be costs involved, both from wastage of base paper and from leaving coating machine capacity spare. The most profitable overall method of programming the production may lie anywhere between these two extremes.

4.7 The Optimum Solution

To choose the best schedule, the relative profitabilities of all possible schedules have to be assessed. This must be done keeping the machine capacities fixed because, with some methods of scheduling, spare capacity may be available for alternative forms of production. The principle is illustrated in Figure 4.3 which considers only one base machine and one coating machine for the two alternative objectives, i.e. minimum paper trim or maximum use of coater capacity. Suppose that the programme is for minimum trim, when the coater produces X tons per week which require Y tons of base paper, made in Z hours on the paper machine. Alternatively, suppose that the programme is designed for maximum use of coater

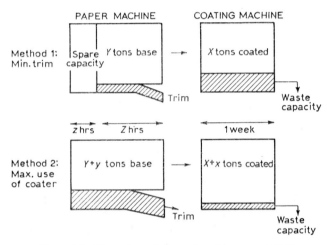

Figure 4.3 Alternative extremes of machine arrangement

capacity. The coater output will now be increased, say to $X + x$ tons per week, requiring $Y + y$ tons of base paper. The time taken to make this base paper will be longer than Z, for two reasons: (i) more base paper is required (an increase of y tons), and (ii) the paper trim loss is larger. If the time required on the paper machine is $Z + z$ hours, alternative allocations of the z hours' production not used by the first allocation must be included in the comparison. Costs can then be properly estimated and the relative profitabilities of the two allocations compared.

Wiggins Teape have applied these principles to a complex system involving three or more mills and a number of machines of various widths. Orders for several different types of paper have to be met, some coated on one side and some on both sides. Two distinct coating mixes are applied by dissimilar coating systems on coating machines of six different sizes (widths) and running speeds. Finishing adds a further variety of equipment, and there is a considerable interchange of base paper and partly coated paper from machine to machine and from mill to mill. All this has to be integrated into one coherent and efficient operation of optimum profitability, bearing in mind the various costs involved. The revised optimum method of allocation will not necessarily be one where the base paper trim is minimized, or the coater capacity utilization is maximized: it may fall somewhere between these two extremes.

Some results of specimen calculations made are shown below for the two extreme methods of planning and for the intermediate method which was found after detailed investigation to be the best amongst a wide range of possibilities examined:

Method	Trim loss on base	Waste coater capacity
(i) Minimum trim loss on base	2%	6%
(ii) Optimum cost	8%	1%
(iii) Maximum use of coater	15%	$\frac{1}{2}$%

A computer program to give the optimum schedule has been developed and its use confirms the above figures. Note that the optimum method is a long way, in its waste and utilization figures, from either of the two extremes of production which might have been used if programming techniques had been applied blindly, and the difference in profitability between the various methods is very substantial. Initially it had been believed that filling the coating capacity would be likely to produce the best results, but the work has shown this to be a fallacy. In fact, this procedure was the worst of those shown in the table and the method finally chosen has enabled an increase in overall profitability of some 5% to be achieved for this particular paper.

4.8   Planning over Time

In many of the illustrations given above, linear programming was used to deduce the optimum allocation of resources at a given moment of time. Planning, for production or investment in the general sense, involves not only decision about which products to make and in what quantity, but also decisions about the choice of raw materials and plant to use, the timing of operations, and whether to buy or hire additional resources such as extra processing or storage capacity. Planning may also include decisions about where to manufacture various products, taking account of availabilities of materials, processing methods and efficiencies at various plants, and the costs of transport of raw materials and of products to customers.

Linear programming can assist with all these problems, coupled as well with the allocation over time. Linear programming cannot be used to forecast future events, and so all estimates of future sales, selling prices, raw material prices and availabilities must be made by other methods. Given such data, the linear programming technique will then provide the optimum solution. For example, if sales are seasonal, a linear programming model can be used to decide how stocks should be built up during the slack season. A company whose sales are seasonal may choose to keep stocks low and work maximum overtime during the busy period, or to build up stocks before the heavy selling season and then work less overtime. Decisions of this kind will depend upon the relative costs of storage and of overtime working, as well as on the storage facilities, plant availabilities and forward sales forecasts.

If there is uncertainty about some or all of the estimates, it is usually possible, once the programme is formulated, to feed in a succession of different estimates and obtain a new optimum solution for each. The resulting set of solutions will then provide a good indication as to how changes in circumstances are likely to affect the company's plan. If some not improbable set of circumstances could cause serious difficulties the company may be able to take appropriate cautionary action in good time.

REFERENCES

Those of Chapter 3 and, in addition, the following:
(1) *Quantitative Approaches to Management* by R. I. Levin and C. A. Kirkpatrick (McGraw-Hill) (Chapter 9).
(2) *Readings in Mathematical Programming* by S. Vajda (Pitman, 1962) (Chapters 2 to 6).
(3) Machine programming by W. S. Harvey and E. Jowett, *The Paper Maker* (1965), Vol. 150, pp. 59–64.
(4) *Linear and Non-linear Programming in Industry* by N. Williams (Pitman, 1967).
(5) *Mathematical Programming in Practice* by E. M. L. Beale (Pitman, 1968).

Some examples of specific applications are:
(6) A case study in mathematical programming of portfolio selections, by N. R. Paine, *Applied Statistics* (1966), Vol. 15, pp. 24–36.
(7) Separable programming applied to an ore purchasing problem, by E. M. L. Beale *et al.*, *Applied Statistics* (1965), Vol. 14, pp. 89–101.
(8) A warehouse location problem, by W. J. Baumol and P. Wolfe, *Operations Research* (1958), Vol. 6, pp. 252–263.
(9) Forest management and operational research—a linear programming study, by P. A. Wardle, *Management Science* (1965), Vol. 11B, pp. 260–270.

5 The Planning of Operations— Queueing

5.1 Introduction

After selecting goods in a supermarket, a shopper must take them to a desk for checking and payment. The customer may be served immediately, or may have to wait for previous customers to be served. Most customers would naturally like to be served immediately, which would imply that there should always be empty desks with cashiers awaiting customers. The store manager, on the other hand, would like to have his cashiers busy all the time. These requirements conflict because customers do not arrive at the desks at fixed and regular intervals, and some take longer to be served than others. If a cashier is to be kept fully occupied, a queue will develop at the desks when customers arrive more frequently than usual, or take longer than usual to be served. If the queues get too long, they will begin to block the shop and customers, finding that they often have a long wait, may decide to shop elsewhere. For this reason the manager would then have to consider employing a further cashier. Obviously this should reduce the customers' waiting times and cut down the queue length, but at the same time it will add to his costs. The manager, in deciding whether to pay for one or more extra cashiers, will want to know the consequential effects on both the average waiting time and the queue length.

The basic features of a problem of this sort are that: there is some form of *input* of units requiring some kind of *service*; this service may not always be immediately available, in which case a *waiting-line* will be formed; when a unit has been serviced it leaves, forming the *output* of the queueing system. This can be shown diagrammatically as in Figure 5.1.

The input in the example above is formed by the customers arriving at the cash desk to pay. If no desk is free they form a queue or waiting line. When a cash desk becomes vacant, the next customer moves forward for payment or service and finally, when each finishes paying for her goods, she leaves the store, forming the output.

A queueing problem arises because of the irregularity of the rate of input or of service, or both, so that input and service cannot be matched exactly in an arithmetic or deterministic fashion. If a cashier always took exactly 20 seconds to deal with a customer and a customer arrived every 20 seconds precisely, then there would be no queue and, correspondingly, the cashier would be 100% occupied. The system could then be said to be 100% effective. If the time taken by the cashier to deal with each customer were reduced from exactly 20 seconds to exactly 18 seconds and the customers still arrived at 20-second intervals, then whilst there would still be no queue, the

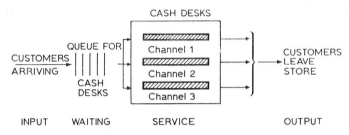

Figure 5.1 Basic queueing situation

cashier would only be 90% (i.e. $\frac{18}{20} \times 100$) occupied. But suppose that the interval between arrivals now varied from 10 seconds to 30 seconds, retaining an average interval of 20 seconds, what effect would this have? A typical short-run situation might then be:

Arrival number	1	2	3	4	5	6	7	8
Inter-arrival times	18	12	19	14	20	28	25	19
Time (cumulative)	18	30	49	63	83	111	136	155
Time into cashier	18	36	54	72	90	111	136	155
Time exit from cashier	36	54	72	90	108	129	154	183
Queueing time	0	6	5	9	7	0	0	0

(All times expressed in seconds.)

Thus a short run of below-average intervals, of a kind which will occur fairly frequently, has quickly led to a queue building up. Even though the cashier, from time 18 through to time 183, is only occupied 144/183 or 78·7% of the time, there is still a total of 27 seconds' waiting time occurring, an average of about $3\frac{1}{2}$ seconds per arrival. If the service time were also found to vary, rather than be a fixed 18 seconds, the degree of queueing could be expected to rise yet further. Thus it is the level of variability, both in the arrival intervals and in the service times, that induces the queueing (in a system that would otherwise appear to be capable of having neatly balanced activities).

One of the earliest examples of this kind of problem arose in connexion with the design of telephone exchanges where the inputs are the callers and the service channels are the lines at the exchange. Anyone with a working knowledge of a small manually operated internal switchboard in an organization will be familiar with the kinds of difficulties that occur. Work on problems of this type was first published by K. Erlang, a Danish engineer, in 1909. He applied his results to a number of problems and, in particular, to estimating the optimum number of channels that should be available from one telephone exchange to another. The detailed solutions of most queueing problems met with in practice are intricate and require heavy mathematics. The present discussion will be confined to illustrating the principles through a number of examples.

5.2   Traffic Intensity

Many queueing problems make use of a quantity called the *traffic intensity*. This is defined as the demand expressed as a proportion of the service capacity, or more explicitly as the average service time divided by the average interval between successive arrivals at the service point. The calculation of the traffic intensity for a single server system is relatively simple. The intervals between the arrivals of individual items at the point of input are measured, and the average of these intervals determined. Next a similar calculation is made for the average service time. The traffic intensity would then be the quotient of these two averages, i.e.

$$\frac{\text{average service time}}{\text{average inter-arrival interval}}$$

For example, a post office counter has an average interval between arrival of customers of 4·8 minutes, whilst the average time taken to serve a customer is 3·2 minutes. Then the traffic intensity, denoted here by the symbol t, will be $t = 3\cdot2/4\cdot8 = 0\cdot67$.

In a simple queueing system with only one service point (and hence only one queue as in the case of a post office with a single clerk serving) a value of t less than one indicates an absence of queues, provided that the service times and arrival intervals do not vary from one occasion to the next. If they do vary, the precise queues generated depend upon the form of the variation, but it has been demonstrated mathematically that, under certain assumptions regarding the variability of service times and arrival intervals, the customer's average total waiting time (including the time being served) will be

$$\frac{1}{1-t} \ \textit{multiplied by} \ \text{the average service time}$$

His average waiting time (excluding for this the time spent in actually being served) will be

$$\frac{t}{1-t} \; multiplied \; by \; \text{the average service time}$$

This relationship is only strictly true over a long period of observation, where the arrival intervals and service times both vary with the particular kind of distribution known as the "negative exponential." This distribution is, however, quite common in queueing situations, so that the relationship provides a reasonable approximation for a large number of practical problems. Applying this to the earlier post office example, the estimated average waiting time would be

$$\frac{1}{1-0.67} \times 3.2 = 9.6 \text{ minutes}$$

of which 3·2 minutes would be for actual service, while 6·4 minutes would be spent waiting for service. This may or may not be considered tolerable, but the fine balance of the system should be noted, in that a marginal increase in demand, with a new average arrival interval of, say, 4·0 in place of 4·8 minutes, raises the average waiting time to 16 minutes, of which the queueing element rises from 6·4 to 12·8. Thus a 17 per cent reduction in the mean arrival interval leads to a doubling of the average waiting time.

In fact, with traffic intensities above 0·7 or so, waiting times increase very rapidly indeed, as Figure 5.2 demonstrates. For any particular traffic intensity the vertical axis gives the ratio of average waiting time to average service time. For example, with a traffic intensity of 0·7 and an average service time of 3 minutes, the average waiting time will be 3 × 2·3 or 6·9 minutes. This is in accordance with the observable fact that bottlenecks arise when a very marginal increase in traffic intensity occurs in systems where the intensity is already high. It should be noted that when the system starts from rest—say at the opening of the post office in the morning—the congestion may take a long while to build up, but once congestion is built up it may be very slow to disperse unless the traffic intensity level can be considerably reduced, for example, by employing extra servers. It is, therefore, wise not to allow the traffic intensity of any servicing point to approach unity unless considerable flexibility is available for reducing it should occasion arise.

5.3   The Avoidance of Bottlenecks

Queueing and allied bottleneck situations that are unacceptable must be examined to see how they can be improved. In the queueing

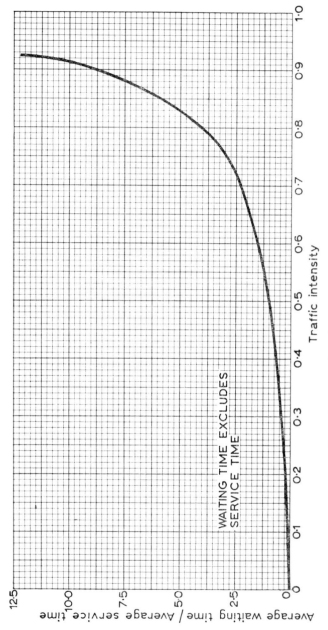

Figure 5.2 Traffic intensity effect on average waiting time

situation illustrated in Figure 5.1 the two factors that could be susceptible to change are

(*a*) the input pattern,
(*b*) the service facilities.

Before examining these factors in detail, however, it ought to be pointed out that some method study of the operation itself may be

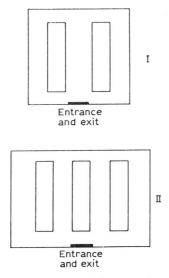

Figure 5.3 Layout of supermarkets

worthwhile, as bottlenecks may be caused purely by poor attention to planning.

Consider the layout of a supermarket and, in particular, the two supermarkets illustrated in Figure 5.3. What is the basic difference between them? The sizes differ, of course, but consider the way in which shoppers will tend to go round the supermarket. In case I there are three aisles only, an odd number. Hence if a customer is to go down *every* aisle, and the layout of goods in a supermarket is usually carefully arranged to try and ensure that this happens, then it follows that he (or more usually she) must go down at least one aisle twice. In practice a bottleneck would probably occur at the top left-hand corner of the supermarket. In case II there are four aisles, an even number. Hence customers could go down every aisle once and arrive back near the exit, without any necessity for repeat visits. The second situation is clearly preferable. Now this problem of layout design—if it is indeed recognized by supermarket planners as a problem—is of a kind which can be solved by a straight-forward study of the system rather than by detailed mathematics.

Reverting to the more common queueing-type situation, sometimes both factors need to be changed, sometimes only one. Indeed it is not always that both are susceptible to change. For example, patients arrive at a doctor's surgery in a fairly random manner and there tend to be large variations in the time intervals between successive arrivals. This variation in arrival intervals could be reduced by having some kind of appointment system whereby there was a predetermined interval between the arrivals of patients, with a consequent reduction in the amount of queueing. The variation in service times, which in this context are actual consultation times by the doctor, are unlikely to be susceptible to any marked modifica-tion. There may be a case for having an extra doctor, or for pro-viding him with nursing assistance to modify his service time distribu-tion, but the basic distribution is likely to be intractable.

It must be realized, too, that the ideal situation is not necessarily one where all queues are eliminated. Frequently this would mean enormous idle time amongst the service facilities, and a balance must be struck between costs of queues and costs of extra servicing facilities. Consider, for example, a port with unloading facilities and ships arriving for unloading in a higgledy-piggledy fashion. The amount of unloading facilities available could be varied and for each level of facilities the total costs computed. Clearly, if there were infinite loading facilities the costs would be infinite (and the waiting zero). As the facilities decrease the costs decrease, but there comes a time when queues of ships start to form and extra costs for demurrage are thereby incurred. As loading facilities are further reduced there comes a point when the saving on an extra marginal decrease in unloading facilities is just outweighed by the extra costs of ships queueing incurred as a consequence. This would provide the overall optimum situation, which is shown schematically in Figure 5.4. The optimum utilization of the unloading facilities will not always be at 60%. It is a function of many factors such as costs of berths, cranes, rate of arrivals of ships, demurrage charges, etc. However, for each set of conditions, there will be some optimum balance which is the point to aim at, and this point of balance will almost certainly envisage some idle time both amongst the ships arriving and amongst the unloading facilities available in the port. In a number of situations the costs of waiting and the costs of the facilities may often be borne—at least initially—by different organiza-tions, so that there may be nobody who is charged with, or indeed interested in, finding the overall optimum.

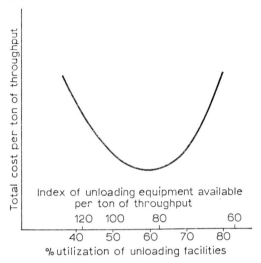

Figure 5.4 Optimum balance of resources

5.4 The Servicing of Machines

The range of queueing problems which can be handled on a straight-forward mathematical basis is not large, for reasons that will be discussed in section 5.6. Nevertheless a great deal of pioneering work has been done using formal mathematical procedures.

To illustrate a queueing problem which can be handled mathematically, consider the following, extracted from a Swedish article by C. Palm (see reference 5 at end of chapter). This article describes the servicing of completely automatic machines that normally require no human attention in their operation. The machines may, however, break down at varying intervals of time and then require servicing. The time needed for servicing a machine once it has broken down is again taken to be variable rather than fixed. Suppose that an individual machine is characterized by the two constants, r and s, where

> r is the average time for the repair of a machine once it has broken down and a man is working on it,

and

> s is the average time between breakdowns of an individual machine.

Let p_n represent the probability that, at any one time, there will be n machines broken down amongst a group of m machines.

TABLE 5.1

Probabilities for Six Machines, One Repair-man

Number of machines broken down (n)	Machines being serviced	Machines awaiting service (excluding machines being serviced)	Probability p_n
0	0	0	0·485
1	1	0	0·291
2	1	1	0·145
3	1	2	0·057
4	1	3	0·018
5	1	4	0·004
6	1	5	0·000
		Total	1·000

Each machine has the same value of r and also the same value of s. A single repair-man is available to service the machines. Palm shows how the values of p_n can be deduced mathematically, once the value of the ratio r/s is fixed. For the illustrative values in Table 5.1 above, it is assumed that there are six machines ($m = 6$) and that the value of the ratio r/s is taken as 0·1 for each machine. Such a ratio would mean, for example, that when considering one individual machine, the average time between breakdowns was 10 hours, but, once it had broken down and was being serviced, the average time for its repair was 1 hour. If both r and s are multiplied by the same factor, then the ratio r/s, and hence the probabilities for p_n, would remain unaltered.

Table 5.1 shows that there will be at least one machine broken down for approximately 51 per cent of the time, i.e. $(1 - 0·485) \times 100$. Furthermore there will be at least one machine waiting in the queue to get attention for about 22 per cent of the time, i.e.

$$(0·145 + 0·057 + 0·018 + 0·004) \times 100$$

The average number of machines broken down and awaiting service at any one time will be the sum of the products of the individual entries in the third and fourth columns of the table, i.e. 0·329. The argument for this is that there is at any moment of time a probability of 0·145 that one machine is awaiting service, or a probability of 0·057 that two machines are awaiting service, etc., so that the average number of machines awaiting service is

$$1 \times 0·145 + 2 \times 0·057 + 3 \times 0·018 + 4 \times 0·004 = 0·329$$

5.5 Generalization of Servicing Problem

The scope of the problem can be widened by assuming that more than one repair-man is available. It is assumed that only one repair-man is needed on each broken-down machine, and so it is logical that there should be no more repair-men than the total number of machines in the system. The amended mathematical equations that arise from the changed conditions still have explicit solutions.

TABLE 5.2

Probabilities for 20 Machines, Three Repair-men

Number of machines broken down (n) (1)	Machines being serviced (2)	Machines awaiting service (excluding machines being serviced) (3)	Repairmen idle (4)	Probabilities p_n (5)
0	0	0	3	0·136
1	1	0	2	0·273
2	2	0	1	0·259
3	3	0	0	0·154
4	3	1	0	0·088
5	3	2	0	0·047
6	3	3	0	0·024
7	3	4	0	0·011
8	3	5	0	0·005
9	3	6	0	0·002
10	3	7	0	0·001
11	3	8	0	0·000

Suppose there are 20 machines and 3 repair-men, then the appropriate values are as tabulated in Table 5.2, the ratio r/s again being taken as 0·1.

From Table 5.2 various calculations and comparisons can be made. If there were 20 repair-men available, so that any machine breaking down would never under any circumstances have to wait for service, the machine efficiency (i.e. proportion of the time for which a machine was open for work that is useful productive time) would be $s/(s + r)$, or 0·91. If there were only three repair-men, then the further fraction of productive time lost could be estimated from the column (5) of Table 5.2 as

$$(1 \times 0·088 + 2 \times 0·047 + 3 \times 0·024 + \ldots)/20 = 0·017$$

since on a fraction 0·088 of occasions there will be one machine awaiting service, on 0·047 of occasions two machines waiting, and so on. The revised machine efficiency is now 0·89 (or 0·91 − 0·017), a small drop at the saving of 17 repair-men.

It is instructive to compare Tables 5.1 and 5.2, since the ratio of arrival interval to service time used is the same in both cases. The ratio of machines to repair-men is slightly higher at 20 machines to 3 repair-men, or 20/3 to 1, in the second table, as opposed to the equivalent ratio of 6 to 1 in the first table. A comparison of the final columns of the two tables does reveal, however, some surprising features which suggest that the repair-men and machines in the situation underlying the second table are being used very much more efficiently. To formulate the differences, consider the following two coefficients:

Machine Loss Coefficient
(MLC)
$$= \frac{\text{Average number of machines awaiting service}}{\text{Number of machines in system}}$$

Repair-men Loss Coefficient
(RLC)
$$= \frac{\text{Average number of repair-men idle}}{\text{Number of repair-men employed}}$$

The numerical values of these coefficients can be calculated from the two tables. For example, from Table 5.1 the MLC for the six-machine situation is equal to

$$(1 \times 0·145 + 2 \times 0·057 + 3 \times 0·018 + 4 \times 0·004)/6 = 0·055$$

whilst the RLC for the first situation is equal to

$$(1 \times 0·485)/1 = 0·485$$

as the single repair-man is only idle when no machines are broken down.

The two situations can then be summarized as in Table 5.3.

Both coefficients are very much lower in the second situation, showing that 3 repair-men servicing a total of 20 machines would be a more economic proposition than having 3 repair-men, each of whom services a separate group of 6 machines. This difference comes about because of the "averaging" effect that is allowed to have more rein in the situation described by Table 5.2. Nevertheless, the difference is a startling one in that the machine loss time has at the same time been drastically cut. It should be noted that if 18 machines were served by 3 repair-men, but divided into three rigid sets of 6 machines to 1 repair-man, with no overlap allowed, then the overall situation would effectively be that shown in Table 5.1.

TABLE 5.3

Comparison of Repair Systems

	Table 5.1 situation	*Table 5.2 situation*
Number of machines	6	20
Number of repair-men	1	3
Machines per repair-man	6	20/3
Machine loss coefficient	0·055	0·017
Repair-men loss coefficient	0·485	0·404

It is only because each of the three repair-men is allowed to service *any* machine in the group which breaks down that the large gains shown have been achieved.

5.6 Alternative Analysis

The systems described in the two foregoing sections were both capable of explicit mathematical analysis. Some systems, however, are so complicated that they defy straightforward mathematical form. For example, the distribution of service times may not follow any well-known statistical distribution that can be written down in straightforward mathematical form. To set about analysing such a situation it is useful to put down once again just what quantities are needed to define a queueing situation in order to build a model to represent the system. For a situation where units arrive (input), are then serviced and finally leave (output), data are needed about:

(i) The distribution of intervals between arrivals,
(ii) The distribution of service times (e.g. how long the cashier takes to add up and take the money),
(iii) The processing or service facilities available (e.g. the number of counters and whether these are all general or have some restriction on the type of service offered),
(iv) The priority system, if any, operated in the queue or waiting line, i.e. the queue discipline which determines whether there is a common queue or a separate one for each service facility.

Given these quantities, a schedule could be written up—maybe rather a lengthy one—of the appropriate times for service and exit for a set of arrivals under the various alternatives which it was desired to investigate, say changes in the service facilities available. This might well be a very laborious procedure for which a digital computer could be of great assistance, but the principle is a simple and straightforward one which goes under the general heading of simulation. This technique is of sufficient importance for the next chapter to be devoted to it. Meanwhile, a straightforward illustration of what is implied by simulation is afforded by the following example relating to the Post Office.

5.7   Post Office Counter Problem

In 1960 a working party carried out some investigations into the relative efficiencies of working the counters in Crown Post Offices using different principles. The two principal methods of working considered here are

(i) *Team working*—counters divided into two categories, banking and stamps. Within these two categories postal officers deal with any item categorized as banking or stamps, but the two types of work do not overlap.

(ii) *Composite working*—a customer entering the office for any class of business (except parcels and one or two specialized transactions) can go to any counter for service.

As a first step a pilot investigation was made concerning the time taken under the existing system of team working then operative in the bulk of Crown offices. For example, at Harrogate Head Post Office the following observations were made:

The Banking team concerned served 634 customers in a period of 739 available "banking minutes," spread over a period of one week. The total waiting (idle) time for the team contained in this study was 185 minutes spread over 202 occasions. Hence the actual average service time per customer was $(739 - 185)/634$, or 0.87 minutes. When a server found himself idle, his idle time lasted on average $185/202 = 0.92$ minutes. Similarly with the Stamp team, 367 customers were studied over a period of 360 minutes. The actual average service time was 0.58 minutes per customer, and there were 187 instances of waiting (idle) time averaging 0.79 minutes per occasion.

Clearly in each team a reserve of service is available equal to some portion of the waiting (idle) time, and this reserve could be utilized provided one team could help the other. Under team working conditions this was virtually impossible, and the enquiry was thus directed into the possibility of using composite working (i.e. breaking up the teams) in offices of this size.

It will be appreciated that the measurement of the results of composite working compared with team working is not a simple arithmetical calculation based on figures such as those quoted above, mainly because of the random pattern of arrival of the customers and the fluctuation in the service times. Short of an actual trial of composite working, it was believed that the construction of a mathematical model to simulate counter operation would be the most beneficial approach and this was done, based on the operations of Colchester Post Office.

The constituents of the queueing situation must first be determined by observation, namely:

(a) The number of servers,

(b) The number of possible queues,

(c) The queue discipline (e.g. whether a customer sticks to the queue he first joins or moves from one queue to another),

(d) The customer "input" expressed as a distribution of intervals between arrivals (estimated by sampling methods),

(e) The service time expressed as a distribution of the length of time taken to serve each customer concerned (estimated by sampling methods).

By means of such information, the actual situation is replaced by a model in the form of a flow diagram. The originally intractable mathematical problem of the effects of alternative methods of operation can now be tackled by simulation techniques. A check can be made against the existing situation by taking observations to determine such quantities as waiting time and queue length and seeing how well these agree with the results from simulations.

Based on a simulation of two hours of counter operations, when 600 customers were served, using identical customer arrival times and service times for both methods of working, Table 5.4 shows the percentage of customers who had to wait for the lengths of time shown in the various bands given in the left-hand column.

The results from Table 5.4 can be alternatively summarized in the comparative form shown in Table 5.5. They show that a considerable reduction in waiting time and queue length would be achieved by a change from team to composite working and, as a consequence, further simulations were carried out and composite working adopted experimentally at a number of Post Offices. Subsequently special tables were computed to show the staffing requirements for different levels of customer arrival rates and service times under composite working.

This illustration shows how simulation provides a method whereby alternative operating systems can be painlessly "lived through" on a piece (or pieces) of paper and all the possible outcomes evaluated before the manager becomes committed to putting any particular

The Planning of Operations—Queueing

TABLE 5.4

Waiting Time Distributions

Waiting time (minutes) over	up to	Percentage of customers Team working	Composite working
	0	47·9	72·5
0	1	18·5	17·0
1	2	9·2	7·2
2	3	7·0	1·0
3	4	6·5	0·9
4	5	2·8	0·8
5	6	2·5	0·3
6	7	3·5	0·3
7	8	1·8	—
8	9	0·3	—
9	—	—	—
		Total 100·0	Total 100·0

scheme into physical operation. The principle has wide applications, some of which are considered in more detail in the following chapter.

TABLE 5.5

Comparative Performance Characteristics

	Team working	Composite working
Average waiting time (minutes)	1·28	0·31
Average queue length	1·78	0·92
Average number of people in office	10·1	5·2

REFERENCES

(1) *Queues, Inventories and Maintenance* by P. M. Morse (Wiley, 1958).
(2) *Queues* by D. R. Cox and W. L. Smith (Methuen, 1961).
(3) *A Guide to Operational Research* by E. Duckworth (Methuen, 1962) (Part II).
(4) *Operations Research* by M. Sasieni, A. Yaspan and L. Friedman (Wiley, 1959) (Chapter 6).
(5) The distribution of repairmen in servicing automatic machines, by C. Palm, *Industritidningen*, Vol. 75, 1947, p. 75.

6 The Planning of Operations—Simulation

6.1 Introduction

The origins of simulation are threefold. First, there has always been a desire to avoid direct experimentation where it is possible. For example, the housewife may rearrange the bedroom furniture by directly experimenting with different layouts. Essentially she (or perhaps her husband under her supervision!) moves the furniture and observes the results. This process may be repeated, and perhaps further moves made, until all logical possibilities have been exhausted. Eventually one such move is judged best, the furniture is returned to this position, and the experiment is completed. Direct experimentation such as this could in theory be applied to the effects of a rearrangement of machinery in a factory. Such a procedure is costly, time-consuming, and disruptive. Hence, simulation, or indirect experimentation, is employed, using a model to represent the factory and templates to represent the items of machinery to be moved. Again direct experimentation in aircraft design would involve constructing a full-scale prototye which could be flight-tested under real conditions. Although this is an essential step at a particular phase in the evolution of a new design, it would be very costly as a first step. The usual procedure is to evaluate several proposed configurations by building a model of each and then testing in a wind tunnel. Again this is the process of simulation.

The second origin lies in the solution of purely mathematical problems in fields such as differential equations. Many mathematical equations can be solved by simulation techniques. For example, a circle with diameter 1 unit has an area, by definition, of $\frac{1}{4}\pi$. Suppose that the value of π is unknown and has to be estimated. One way to do this would be to surround such a circle with a square of unit side, as shown in Figure 6.1. Next, take a point at random in the area defined by the square. The probability that this point lies in the circle is simply the ratio of the two areas. The square has area 1, and by definition the area of the circle is π multiplied by the square of the radius, i.e. $\frac{1}{4}\pi$. Hence the probability of falling in the circle is $\frac{1}{4}\pi/1$, or $\frac{1}{4}\pi$. If a large number of points are taken at random within the square area, then the proportion of these points also lying in the circle is an estimate of $\frac{1}{4}\pi$. Hence, the use of random selection techniques provides an experimental means of finding a numerical value that is needed and which would otherwise require complicated, if not intractable, mathematics for its determination. Many of the problems falling into this category are tremendously complex, for example the determination of the critical size of a nuclear reactor.

The third origin lies in the growth of operational research. One

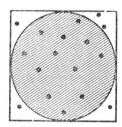

Figure 6.1 Evaluation of π

outstanding difference between the subject-matter of much conventional scientific research and operational research is characterized by the greater variability of many of the phenomena studied in the latter. It was vital to bring regularity back into the description of these phenomena—to find a usable description of the variability. This was achieved, as had been done for actuarial science and economics in the previous century, by the use of probability theory. Once again the investigator turned to an experimental technique. Operational problems were phrased in a real world language involving queues, stocks, machines, and operating instructions. The technique of considering alternatives in an experimental manner was named simulation and yet, as has been explained, it was really nothing new. To a statistician, the problem was closely akin to finding the sampling distribution of an intricately and irregularly defined statistic, and, because of the intricate nature of the system concerned, having to do this by a sampling procedure. In operations economy, the objective sought is the maximization of an economic measure of effectiveness. Rarely, if ever, can this be done by direct experimentation with the operations under study. For example, a sales price which maximizes profit cannot be determined by actually changing the price over a range of values until the optimum price level is located. Such a method is expensive, time-consuming, and, in addition, may eventually destroy the price structure itself. Hence operational policies are usually established by intuition, judgment, and simulation rather than by direct experimentation.

6.2 The Monte Carlo Technique

A standard technique of random selection is the system commonly referred to as the Monte Carlo technique, linked to the gambling casinos rather than the car rally. To illustrate the principles, a simple example will be described. Consider a new product which contains two independent and distinct parts, each of which will eventually fail. These parts might be a condenser and a vacuum tube. From past tests and records, the probability of failure of each item in terms of its time in use has been estimated, i.e. the life curve of each item is available. What is wanted is the life curve of the product which contains one of each of these elements—assuming the product fails when the first component fails. Denote the original life distributions of the components by the symbols f and g respectively, whilst the symbol h denotes that of the combined derived distribution. Now in some cases h can be derived by mathematical analysis. This will occur when f and g can be represented by simple mathematical functions. But in other instances it is not possible or practical to evaluate the derived function h in this way. In such instances the Monte Carlo technique may be the best method available.

Assume that the frequency of incidence of time to failure of the two components is as shown in Figure 6.2. In the assembly of the product, one item from each class of component will be selected at random. To simulate this, items must be selected in such a way that each has an equal chance of being selected. Since there are clearly more items of the first component with life spans in some intervals (say the interval from 95 to 105) than in other intervals (say the interval from 75 to 85), the procedure must be such that the chance of selecting an item in any chosen interval on the time scale is equal to the proportion of items falling in that interval. Now a simple random sample drawn from the set of possible time values laid out along the horizontal axis would lead to giving the same chances to the drawing of an item with a life span between 95 to 105 as to one between 75 and 85. This is clearly an inflexible and incorrect procedure. Hence a technique must be devised for sampling from frequency distributions, taking into account the relative frequencies of the different intervals. One time-honoured way of doing this is by drawing discs from a drum. The discs would have numbers on them representing the possible values of the variable (e.g. time)

concerned. To achieve the necessary weighting of the values of this
variable, the number of discs given any particular value would need
to be proportional to the frequency with which such a value occurs
in the frequency distribution in question. In theory a large number
of discs would be needed, to ensure sufficiently good representation
of the distribution, and the discs must be well shuffled before each
drawing to ensure that each disc stands an equal chance of being
selected. To obtain a series of values for the variable concerned, a

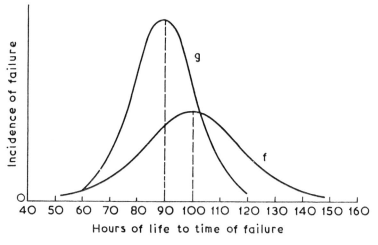

Figure 6.2 Distribution of component lives

series of discs would be drawn, each drawn disc being replaced and
the drum reshuffled before the next disc is drawn.

An alternative method of achieving the same result would be to
take a roulette wheel, with a mark on one point of the inner spinning
circumference, and to segment the outer numbered circumference in
proportion to the chances required for different lengths of life.
For example, the segment of circumference applicable to the interval
95 to 105 would be about twice as long as that applicable to the
interval 75 to 85. The wheel can now be spun and the life of the
first component found by noting the interval opposite which the
mark stops. A separate wheel is required for the second component
with a different, but appropriate, segmentation of the outer circumference. This wheel is now spun and the life of the second component found. The life of the product is the lesser of these two lengths
of life. The whole procedure would now be repeated a large number
of times, using the same two calibrated wheels, so as to formulate

the distribution of life of the product. The resulting distribution for *h* is of the form shown in Figure 6.3. To obtain a distribution as smooth as that shown would require a large number of simulations, and the jagged dotted distribution shows the form that it might have

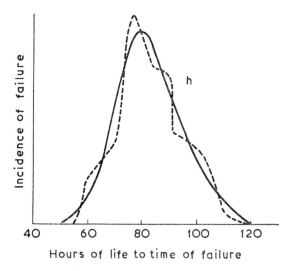

Figure 6.3 Distribution of combined product lives

reached at a somewhat earlier stage. Note that these techniques can be applied whatever the shape of the original distributions of component lives. The distributions do not have to be smooth and bell-shaped as shown, but could equally well be of an irregular form.

6.3 Drawing the Sample

In practice the shuffling or wheel spinning can be avoided by visualizing each disc as bearing a serial number, as well as the value of the variable. The random selection then turns on ensuring that the serial numbers of the discs chosen are a random sample. This can be taken a stage further and for the drum of numbered discs a table of values of random variables, each one numbered serially, can be substituted. To apply this Figure 6.4 (which is an approximate representation of component *g* from Figure 6.2) shows the variable *g* being allotted serial numbers according to the frequency of each value, with the lower-values of the variable being allocated the lower serial numbers. In the figure the only critical points now are those serial numbers with which a new value of the variable *g* is associated.

This enables the so-called histogram of Figure 6.4 to be turned into the following rather simple tabular form:

Value of g	65	70	75	80	85	90	95	100	105	110	115	120
Lowest serial number	1	2	5	9	14	22	32	39	44	47	49	50

The serial number scale could be changed so that it ran from 0 to 1 instead of 1 to 50, by dividing all numbers by 50. The problem has

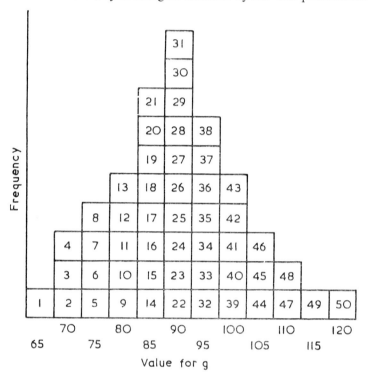

Figure 6.4 Random sampling skeleton

then been reduced, by a common mathematical trick, so that sampling from any defined distribution is put in terms of the simpler and more general problem of selecting random numbers in the range 0 to 1. If a method is available for the latter problem, it can accordingly be generalized to cover sampling from any distribution.

A sequence of random numbers (or more precisely a random sequence of the digits 0 to 9) may be used to give the decimal representations (to a desired degree of precision) of the members of a random sample in the range 0 to 1. Randomness is not a function of the numbers themselves (which is the more random, 7 or 4?), but a function of sequences of numbers, i.e. their inter-relationships. If a sequence of numbers is truly random, the knowledge of what the $(n + 1)$th value is likely to be is not improved by knowledge of the past history of the sequence up to and including the nth value. But since sequences which produce marked patterns may occur (however infrequently) in an infinite series of numbers chosen at random, it must be the process of choosing that defines the randomness of the sequence rather than the numbers themselves. Thus randomness is a function of the device that produces the sequence of numbers concerned. But why this concern with randomness? It is because in so many cases independence is assumed between certain variables in the models of real life operations that are being examined. The randomness is an imperfect representation, born of ignorance, and hence does not itself generally have to be perfect. Ideally at any point of the sequence each number should be equally likely to occur, irrespective of the pattern of numbers earlier in the sequence.

Since many simulations are large-scale affairs, vast quantities of random numbers are needed and the use of computers becomes important. Now the computer is a strictly deterministic device and as such is incapable of generating truly random numbers, which would therefore have to be stored in the computer or fed in every time they were required. With maybe a million or more of these numbers, such approaches are inconvenient and costly in practice. The solution is the generation of "pseudo-random" numbers within the computer. This means that some arithmetic rule is used to compute each number from earlier numbers of the sequence, the rule being chosen in such a way that the numbers obtained appear to be random. This method has the advantage that each member of the sequence can be calculated quickly when it is needed, and the whole sequence is reproducible with only a few numbers having to be stored at any one time.

6.4 The Rolling Mill

This illustration of the simulation process relates to a problem where a rolling mill has material waiting to be rolled, thus forming a queue. It is a particular case of a single server queue with variable service times and arrival intervals, for the time (t_1) between arrivals of material and the time (t_2) taken to process it once it is in the rolling mill are probabilistic. In a simulation model these times have, therefore, to be generated as samples from their respective probability distributions (which might be obtained by gathering facts from the real-life situation. Figure 6.5 illustrates the situation, and the corresponding distributions of the times t_1 and t_2.

The distribution of service times in the rolling mill will be independent of the size of the queue of raw material. A known distribution of process times for the furnace allows the times for t_2 to be estimated, and hence the output times from the system can be determined. An item of raw material will be taken from the queue

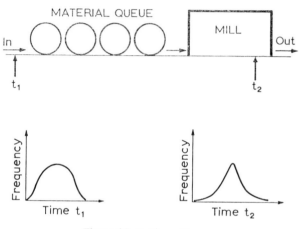

Figure 6.5 Rolling mill queue

into the mill in accordance with some rule. This rule describes the "queue discipline." There are basically three possible rules:

FIFO (first in, first out)
LIFO (last in, first out)
Random selection from the waiting queue

The optimum solution to such a problem could depend upon the viewpoint taken. The works manager's aim would no doubt be to reduce the size of the queue; the queue discipline used would be immaterial. From the point of view of the rolling mill machinery the aim would be to reduce idle time to a minimum; queue discipline again being irrelevant. Finally if the items themselves were cooling steel (and heat is money) they would have as their aim the reduction in the total time taken for service.

Adopting the works manager's criterion as the most desirable, note that the queue size changes only when there is an arrival or a departure. Therefore using this approach the rest of the time (in which all the real work is done) is of no interest to the simulator, who need only consider the system at the times when such an event occurs.

6.5 The Simulation Model

The flow diagram shown in Figure 6.6 describes a simulation model of the rolling mill, which will record the largest queue occurring in a given length of time.

At the start of a simulation run the initial state of the system must be set up. In this case it was assumed that initially there was no queue and no material was being processed. To give this initial state the current queue length Q and the time T_2 of the next departure from the mill are both set to zero. The time T_1 at which the next arrival occurs is taken initially as a sample from the distribution of arrival intervals t_1. The initial conditions are completed by setting the largest queue size recorded, n, to zero and setting the total time L it is required to simulate.

At each stage of the simulation the nature of the next event to occur is determined by comparing the values of T_1 and T_2. If it is an arrival then the right-hand fork of the diagram will be taken and the current queue length increased by 1. The largest queue length n is updated if necessary, and the time of the next arrival is calculated by sampling from t_1. The simulation is halted, after the appropriate data has been obtained, as soon as the next arrival time T_1 becomes greater than L; at this stage the time limit has not yet been exceeded while no more arrivals can occur within it.

When a departure is to occur the left-hand fork is taken and the queue length decreased by 1. If there was currently no queue then the mill becomes idle and must wait for the next arrival. In this case the next departure time T_2 is calculated by adding a sample from the distribution of service times t_2 to the next arrival time T_1. If there was already a queue then the sample is added to current departure time.

Such flow diagrams are usually written with the computer in mind and are normally straightforward to program. If the total waiting time under various queue disciplines was required, then again simulation could be used. In this case the corresponding flow diagram would be more complicated and more variables would have to be stored at each stage.

6.6 Unloading at a Port

A second illustration of queueing, which was briefly mentioned in Chapter 1, is taken from an interesting paper by Page and Steer (see reference 5 at end of chapter) concerned with the operations of an iron-ore unloading port. The scope of the work was primarily to determine whether the port could be modified to handle the estimated future foreign ore requirements. Basically the objective was concerned with the financial and operational advantages that would accrue if the entrance channel to the dock were deepened through dredging operations, thereby reducing the dock's physical limitations and the incidence of tidal delays. Having formulated a suitable model to describe the operations of this particular port, the objective was then extended to include both the estimation of the capacity of the system under current conditions as well as the increase in capacity that could be expected from relatively inexpensive modifications. These modifications would incorporate a deeper entrance channel together with reduced service times that might be derived from the application of a method study of the unloading operations at the wharf itself.

Various basic pieces of information were obtained, such as the arrival pattern of the ships, by size as well as by time, the delays that occurred outside the lock, the service times once the ships had arrived at the unloading quay, and the pattern and height of the tides.

In the first instance, attempts were made to obtain a formal mathematical solution. Several mathematical models were formulated but failed to reproduce current or future conditions accurately enough when tested against wharf records and the results of hand simulations. The reason for these failures was that mathematical formulations could not adequately incorporate the wide variety of ships visiting the wharf, the sporadic nature of their arrivals, or the operating methods of the lock which connected the dock to the sea. For this reason Monte Carlo simulation techniques turned out to be essential. A flow diagram of the complete programme of operations was drawn up and a basic procedure for generating arrivals was compiled. To effect the random sampling involved in carrying out the simulation, it was found convenient from the programming point of view to follow the concept of generating pseudo-random numbers internally in the manner mentioned above, rather than to store random numbers in the machine. At the commencement of a run on the computer, the program, together with the data relating to the various relationships and distributions, was fed into the machine and stored. On initiating the program, the data for four tides contained on the arrival tape were read in and processed. This took about 43 seconds and was repeated until the data for some 700 tides had been processed. The computer then printed out the following information for each ship when it had been unloaded: type of ship; arrival tide; hours neaped (i.e. waiting for a tide high enough for the ship to enter the dock); hours queued; berth hours; turn-round time (tides); and cargo weight (tons).

At the end of each simulated week the berth occupancy was

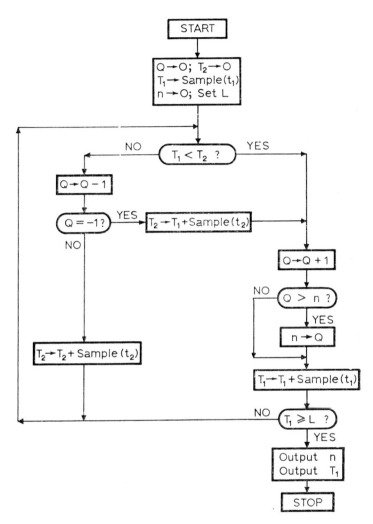

Figure 6.6 Flow diagram

Q = current size of queue

n = largest size queue recorded

L = length of time to be simulated

T_1, T_2 = times in and out of the system, respectively

calculated as a percentage, whilst at the end of each simulated year a great deal more information was printed out relating to the ship-hours lost through various causes, the turn-round times, service times, etc., and the tonnage of ore actually imported. It is interesting to note that the ratio of simulated to actual time achieved with this computer program once it was written proved to be approximately 1:4,200, which may be compared with approximately 1:35 for earlier simulations that were done by hand. This gain would in itself have been sufficient justification of the decision to use the computer in this context, apart from the fact that the program could, without much difficulty, be made to cater for future changes in the various constants of the model.

The results obtained from the simulation showed that the company would gain significant financial and operational benefits by deepening the entrance channel. Further, the present system of use was shown to be incapable of handling the required future changes in throughput without considerable capital expenditure to change the nature of the dock concerned.

6.7 General Business Simulation

As shown above, simulation is a method of approaching a problem by constructing a model of a real situation and then manipulating this model in such a way as to draw some conclusions about the real situation. Simulation, therefore, is not a specific problem-solving technique as such, but an approach to a problem. It demonstrates very vividly all the power of the operational research approach but, because of its wide applicability, simulation can take many and various forms. Nevertheless there are a number of reasons why managers should be familiar with the technique. It has great potential for helping top management, whereas many of the other mathematical techniques apply principally to operating management. Managerial judgment is needed in the development of the model because the typical model-builder does not generally have an intimate enough knowledge of the business to select the appropriate relationships for inclusion in the model. Naturally, too, if management is to make use of simulation models, it must be aware of the principal assumptions that were made in their construction.

The mathematical processes employed in the general business simulation are normally very simple, although this is not to say that building a general business simulation is easy. The typical business is so complex that only a very involved model can come even close to approximating reality. This degree of complexity in itself makes model-building very difficult. Even the most complex model can only include a fraction of the things that are happening in a typical business and, consequently, it is necessary to simplify real life in nearly every part of the model. It takes considerable skill to simplify to the extent that is necessary in the typical model and yet retain reality. The model is also only as good as the values that are placed on the coefficients of the equations, and the determination of these values takes considerable skill. Because of the comparative simplicity of the techniques, many people think that they are capable of building a complex model. This is not true and because the cost of such a model can be quite high, management would be well advised to consider carefully the personnel available before approving a project to develop any general business models.

6.8 Impact of Simulation on Management

Simulation may be used to help top management in strategic planning, as the examples given above demonstrate. It may also be used, as shown in the next chapter, to help operating management in problems such as inventory control policy. A wide difference of opinion exists amongst managers, operational research workers, and simulation experts as to the ultimate potential of the general business simulation. Some believe that it can solve all problems, whilst others believe that business is so complex that it will never be possible to simulate it accurately enough to provide a basis for dependable decisions. The truth probably lies somewhere between these two extremes. Almost without exception, companies that have attempted to build a general simulation model have found that they have benefited indirectly in that the simulation has brought out areas where information systems and planning can be improved. Conflicts arise when the model is to be used for strategic decision-making. The accuracy of the model cannot generally be proved in an absolute sense; the model is most valuable when it results in a manager taking a different decision from that which he would have taken under intuition alone; hence, some resistance to the action indicated may well occur, as it could appear to be attacking the manager's intuitive skills.

The use of a simulation model in improving strategic decision-making will be dependent upon the number of important variables that need to be considered in a particular problem. If only one or two variables influence the entire result, it is evident that the answer provided by the simulation will be directly dependent upon the values placed on these variables. In introducing a new product line, for example, the key variable is usually the volume of sales. The assumptions concerning sales volume will, therefore, determine the answer to a considerable extent.

Simulation models for the operations of a complete organization may be expensive to develop. Hence it is likely that, for the near future, such simulation models will be limited to relatively large companies. Small businesses are unlikely to have the necessary resources for such developments, although if they can divert the necessary resources there may be a large pay-off in following the actions indicated by the application of such models.

REFERENCES

(1) *The Art of Simulation* by K. D. Tocher (English Universities Press, 1963).
(2) *Industrial Dynamics* by J. W. Forrester (M.I.T. Press).
(3) *Cybernetics and Management* by S. Beer (English Universities Press, 1959).
(4) *Management Information Systems* by J. Dearden and F. W. McFarlan (Irwin) (especially Chapter 5).
(5) Feasibility and financial studies of a port installation, by A. C. C. Page and D. T. Steer, *Operational Research Quarterly* (1961), Vol. 12, pp. 145–160.

7 Inventory and Stock Control

7.1 Introduction

Holding stock, in whatever form, costs money. The capital tied up by the stock itself has to be serviced by the payment of interest, and the land or warehouse needed for the stock has to be bought or rented. The handling and securing of the stock, and any quality deterioration that occurs, also cost money. Global figures of actual stocks held in Great Britain are given in the *Monthly Digest of Statistics*. At the end of 1966 the amounts were: Materials and fuel, £2,316 m; Work in progress, £2,511 m; Finished goods, £1,866 m; an overall total of £6,693 m. The total value today is probably even higher but, taken at this figure, the annual cost of holding this stock must exceed £700 m and there is clearly a great incentive to keep stocks to an absolute minimum. Planning the correct amount of stock needed in a factory complex can be complicated, although the principles concerned are straightforward.

Many rules of thumb are operated by companies to control their stocks. For instance, one company has a rule which states that the quantity of any product to be carried in inventory (stock) should be kept (approximately) equal to the amount that customers normally buy in sixty days (or some other fixed period). Such crude rules as this one often exhibit serious shortcomings and could result in excess stocks of some items and insufficient stocks of others. Most businessmen will recognize these rules of thumb for what they are—rough but serviceable management tools—but it is nevertheless worth considering whether such a rule cannot be refined.

7.2 The Square-root Formula

Suppose a manufacturer confidently expects to sell Q units of one of his commodities at a predetermined price over the next year, with the demand spread evenly over the year. How much stock should he keep on hand? Clearly he could stock up with a batch of Q units made at the beginning of the year and sell it evenly over the year. The average stock in hand over the year as a whole would then be $\frac{1}{2}Q$, corresponding to the actual stock held midway through the year. Alternatively he could arrange for monthly mailings of $\frac{1}{12}Q$ and his average stock then becomes $\frac{1}{24}Q$, but he has twelve orderings to arrange and check in per year with all the attendant set-up costs. Figure 7.1 illustrates the situation. Indeed, by having more and more frequent orders the average stock level in hand can be made as low as desired. A lower average stock, of course, saves money on carrying costs (storage, deterioration, interest on capital, etc.) but, on the other hand, there are re-order costs involved in

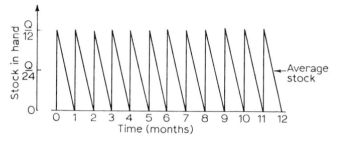

Figure 7.1 Monthly stock pattern

placing, setting up, and delivering an order. Since a smaller stock involves more frequent orders and deliveries, the re-order costs may become prohibitive if management decides upon too small an average stock level.

In practice it is never deliberately planned to allow the stocks to run out altogether, as is tacitly assumed in the foregoing analysis, since unexpected demands or delays in deliveries could be embarrassing. In the formal analysis that follows some minimum extra safety or buffer stock level B could be added throughout the year to allow for this possibility. The choice of value for B is discussed later in the chapter. Such an allowance does not, however, affect the immediate analytical results derived below.

To find the optimal stock level (the level which results in minimum overall cost) mathematical expressions are required for the two types of cost, carrying and re-ordering:

(a) Carrying cost
The average stock level is one-half the amount received in a shipment. Thus if the quantity delivered to the retailer is D units per shipment and demand is evenly spread over time, the average stock level must be

$$\tfrac{1}{2}D$$

Let k be the variable cost of stocking one item for a year calculated as the interest on capital tied up plus other carrying costs involved in holding one item of stock for a year. Then the total carrying cost per annum will be

$$\tfrac{1}{2}Dk \tag{i}$$

(b) Re-order cost
Generally, if Q items are to be sold per annum and there are D items in each delivery made on re-ordering, the required number of deliveries per annum is Q/D. Suppose the cost per delivery is represented by

$$r + sD$$

where r and s are some numbers. The number s may be interpreted as the variable cost per item, whilst r represents the fixed costs per order. For a producer mailing in batches their costs would mainly be the set-up cost per run. For a retailer their costs would be associated with book-keeping, telephoning, checking, etc. The total annual re-ordering cost is now

$$(\text{cost per delivery}) \times (\text{number of deliveries})$$

$$= (r + sD)\frac{Q}{D} \quad \text{or} \quad \frac{rQ}{D} + sQ \tag{ii}$$

The total cost that the manufacturer lays out on his stock is the sum of the two costs (i) and (ii) giving

$$C = \tfrac{1}{2}Dk + \frac{rQ}{D} + sQ \tag{iii}$$

Now the only unknown in equation (iii) will be the value of D as Q, r and k need to be fixed by the conditions of the problem. Once D is determined the inventory situation is completely fixed. With equation (iii) available the solution is, therefore, reduced to a simple one of computation. For example, suppose

$$Q = 200 \qquad k = 8 \qquad r = 20 \qquad s = 3$$

leading to the cost equation

$$C = 4D + \frac{4{,}000}{D} + 600 \tag{iv}$$

Trial and error could now be used to solve equation (iv) and specimen values found as follows:

D	10	20	30	40	50	60
C	1,040	880	853·3	860	880	906·7

Examination of this table and the associated Figure 7.2 suggests (correctly) that the minimum value of C occurs when D is about 32. Thus the equation provides an objective function enabling the problem to be solved.

An extra piece of mathematical analysis, however, enables a

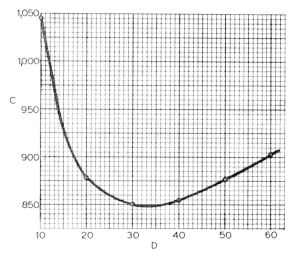

Figure 7.2 Optimum value of D

generalization to be made which avoids the use of trial and error methods to solve equation (iv). This mathematics leads to a further equation, deduced from (iii), which states as a perfectly general result that the optimal value of D, i.e. the value of D which minimizes the cost in equation (iii) is given by

$$\sqrt{\left(\frac{2rQ}{k}\right)} \qquad\qquad\text{(v)}$$

This result is no longer tied to any particular set of numbers, but can be used perfectly generally for any set of values for r, Q and k. Note that s, the variable cost, does not enter into the expression. Substitution of the appropriate figures for this particular example gives 31·6, or 32 to the nearest integer, as deduced graphically.

7.3 Sensitivity of the Result

What is surprising, but important, about the result is that the general formula (v) indicates that the stock level should only increase in proportion to the square root of the sales. Thus the rule of thumb quoted earlier would, even if the total level of stocks held for a variety of products were right, lead to excessive stocks of the popular large sales volume items, and insufficient stocks of the goods whose sales are relatively modest.

A few further practical comments can be made. The optimal formula contains three quantities, namely r, Q and k. Although these should, in theory, be susceptible to accurate estimation this may not really be so in practice. Concentrate attention on r as an illustration. This quantity r is the fixed cost of placing an order for items. As such it represents the costs that are broadly invariant with the size of the order, the machine set-up costs, the checking procedures, and so forth. Such costs may, in fact, not be so easy to estimate as might be anticipated at a first glance. It is, therefore, of interest to see what effect any errors made in the estimation of r would have on the cost structure of the optimal stock policy. Suppose, therefore, that it is assumed that $r = 20$, whereas, in fact, the value of r is really $r' = 40$. The values of $Q = 200$ and $k = 8$ are assumed to be known without error. Now under the assumption that $r = 20$, the re-order quantity will be 32 and the true annual cost, from equation (iii), will be

$$C = \tfrac{1}{2} \times 32 \times 8 + \frac{40 \times 200}{32} + 600$$

$$= 978 \qquad \text{(vi)}$$

But the *true* optimum value of D, using $r' = 40$, is

$$\sqrt{\frac{2 \times 40 \times 200}{8}} = 45 \text{ (approx.)}$$

from equation (v) and the annual cost of stockholding would then be

$$C = \tfrac{1}{2} \times 45 \times 8 + \frac{40 \times 200}{45} + 600$$

$$= 957 \cdot 8 \qquad \text{(vii)}$$

The difference between (vi) and (vii) is 20·2 or about 2%. Hence an "error" of minus 50% in the estimation of r has only affected the total costs by 2%. This may still be a lot of money in absolute terms but, nevertheless, this stability should be borne in mind when judging how far to strive in the quest for accuracy in the quantities to be inserted in the formulae concerned. It must not be surmised from this calculation that the mathematical model has little or no use, rather that the method irons out inconsistencies in the treatment of the various items which need to be included and throws up the relative importance of the different items to be included.

7.4   Re-order Levels

The next stage of development is to consider the re-order level, i.e. the level to which the stock is allowed to fall before a fresh order is placed, as well as the amount of stock that is then ordered. In the preceding section it was tacitly assumed that at the end of each period the stock could be allowed to run out, be replenished instantaneously, and then allowed to run out again, and so on. In practice, sales vary, replenishments are delayed, stocks deteriorate, perish, or go out of vogue. Uncertainty enters the system so that it is no longer strictly deterministic, but essentially *stochastic*. "Stochastic" comes from a Greek word meaning marksman and, just as the archer's arrows group themselves round the bull's eye, so the weekly sales figures will vary, but group themselves round some average level.

The following simple example illustrates a problem relating to the stocking of raw material at a manufacturer, some basic quantities being defined first. Variations occur in demand and in the lead-time and the buffer stock is the amount of extra stock that is kept in the system over and above what would otherwise be required to cater for these variations. The lead-time is the time taken for replenishments to arrive once they have been ordered. A special delivery charge is made if a stock run-out occurs and an emergency supply has to be obtained. What is the stocking system that minimizes the total costs? The relevant data are as follows:

Purchase price per article	£1
Average consumption per week	10 (distributed so that individual weeks vary in their consumption from 4 to 16, with a peak frequency at 10 and frequencies tailing off on either side).
Lead time (days)	14 (distributed so that the time varies from 12 to 16 days, with a peak frequency at 14 days and frequencies tailing off on either side).
Cost of placing an order	10 shillings (£0·5).
Stock-holding costs	20 per cent of value of stock per annum.
Special delivery charge when stock run-out occurs	£5

Using the square-root formula, with a year as the basic time interval, the appropriate re-order quantity will be

$$D = \sqrt{\frac{2 \times 0·5 \times 520}{0·2 \times 1}} = 51$$

Hence the amount to re-order each time is 51. The remainder of the problem revolves around finding the re-order level R, i.e. the level to which the stock falls for a fresh order of 51 items to be made. This level has to cater for both a variable demand and a variable lead-time and will equal the average demand in the average lead-time, plus some buffer stock to allow for the variations in demand and lead-time. If Q is the average demand per unit time, L the average lead-time, and B the buffer stock, then

$$R = Q \times L + B$$

The larger B is made, the smaller will be the chance of running out of stock, but the larger will be the capital tied up. Hence the problem is now reduced to one of minimizing the combined cost of holding the buffer stock B, together with the run-out cost.

The number of orders placed per year is $520/51 = 10 \cdot 2$. If the probability, at each repetition of the order/demand cycle, of a stock run-out occurring is p, then the expected or average number of stock run-outs per year is $10 \cdot 2p$.* The expected cost of stock run-outs per year will then be £5 $\times$ $10 \cdot 2p = $ £51p. The cost of holding the buffer stock will be approximately $0 \cdot 2B$, since the stock-holding cost k is equal to 20 per cent of £1. The cost (£) that has now to be minimized is the sum of the two costs, namely

Stock run-out cost + Buffer stock-holding cost $= 51p + 0 \cdot 2B$

$$\text{(viii)}$$

7.5 Choice of Buffer Stock

The size of B which makes the last expression a minimum is required. Figure 7.3 illustrates a typical kind of situation which arises, giving the relative frequency or incidence of demand during the nominal lead-time L. The average is, by definition, $Q \times L$, but there are considerable variations about this level and on some occasions the actual demand observed is higher and, on some occasions, lower. If a buffer stock of size B were held, it would imply that only on those occasions where the demand in the cycle exceeded ($Q \times L + B$) would there be a stock run-out. Against this, however, an extra B units would have to be held more or less permanently in stock. If B were reduced, then the proportion of occasions on which a stock run-out would occur would be increased, but the holding of extra buffer stock would be reduced. Hence as B increases, the value of p reduces, and vice versa. For a particular situation, as in that defined in the last section, the combined cost expression (viii)

---

* Appendix B summarizes the statistical concepts concerning variability and expected values that are utilized in the rest of this chapter and in Chapter 8.

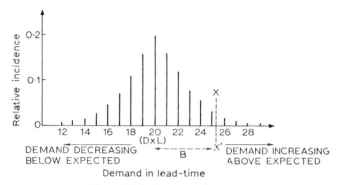

Figure 7.3 Buffer stock distribution

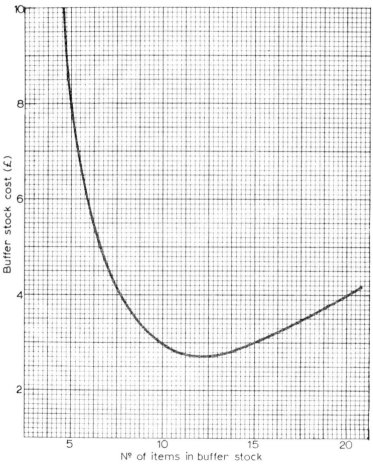

Figure 7.4 Choice of buffer stock

98

above, can be calculated mathematically for various values of B and a graph plotted of cost against B. This is done in Figure 7.4 and from it the optimum buffer stock for this particular situation is read off as 12 items. Since the average demand in the average lead-time is $Q \times L$ which is 20 items, the re-order level is 12 + 20 or 32 items. The lowest possible overall cost is then obtained by re-ordering 51 items every time the stock falls to 32 items. If this system is followed the value of p that has been imputed, from equation (viii) above, is 0·008, i.e. the expected number of run-outs per annum is 12 × 0·008 or 0·09.

7.6 Safety Stocks and Service

In the illustration just discussed, the cost of running out was defined in terms of money. This enabled all the various elements of the inventory system to be put on a common footing. However, this is not always the case, and commonly the level of customer service is expressed in terms of a percentage, such as 90 per cent service or 95 per cent service.

Suppose the re-order level of some inventory system is 57 pieces, and this was chosen because there is a 10 per cent chance that demand during the two month lead-time will exceed 57. The other 90 per cent of the time there is enough stock. Thus the service percentage might be thought of as 90 per cent.

But suppose that a delivery of 25 pieces was received roughly once per month under the ordering rule. The expected or average quantity short in one delivery/order cycle could be studied, and suppose it averaged 0·5 pieces (quite reasonably in line with the figures given). The shortage would average 0·5/25 of the total demand, or 2·0 per cent. Under this method of scoring, the same order rule would give 98 per cent service. Hence by one definition there is 90 per cent service (one chance in ten that a shortage will occur) whilst in the second there is 98 per cent service (only 2 per cent of demand is subject to delay in supply).

A customer who orders a part from the warehouse expects to have the order filled promptly. He knows that there may occasionally be delays caused by shortage, but they can't be allowed to happen too often. The customer doesn't know, and doesn't care, how the stock is managed. Hence in practice it is desirable to give customers the same chance of finding what they want in stock when they want it and to judge the quality of service by the first rule.

Basically the safety stock required, under either rule, is proportional to the product of two factors

$l \times v$

where *l* represents the level of service it is desired to give and *v* represents the degree of variability in the forecast demand for the item during the lead-time. For a given level of service, the safety stock is proportional to the variability in demand, and vice versa. If variability is expressed in terms of standard deviation (see Appendix B) then there are tables available (see reference 4 from R. G. Brown at end of chapter) which will provide the value of *l* in terms of

  D   Number of pieces per order placed,
  M   Service (probability of filling order),
  v   Standard deviation of forecast demand for item during lead-time.

For example, if $D = 15$, $v = 8.5$, $M = 98$ per cent, then *l* is found mathematically to be 1·4 and the safety stock is $1.4 \times 8.5 = 11.9$. This safety stock of 12 would be added to the normal stock required to meet demand during the lead-time in order to determine the order point.

7.7   Centralized Stores

Many organizations have one or more central stores and a large number of branch stores. The hospital service, for example, has some central storehouses and depots in the country, and subsidiary storehouses in the individual hospitals fed from the central stores.

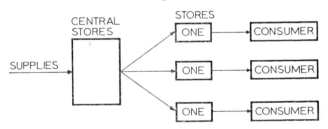

Figure 7.5a   Centralized store system

A large company may have one big central stores organization with separate stores at factory or plant level, as illustrated in Figure 7.5(*a*).

In such types of organization there is the problem of deciding which items should be centrally, as opposed to universally, stocked and how often items centrally held should be distributed to the subsidiary stores. Very often centralized store holdings can lead to economies in the level of overall stock-holding, and in the operation of the stores, as well as achieving better care of the material. In such instances, factors militating against central stores would be the poorer availability of goods on demand at the peripheral locations, and added transport costs to fulfil some requests. In any given situation it should be possible to enumerate the factors for and against, and to deduce conditions which determine the optimum location of the items to be held. The problem in its essence is the typical optimization problem of balancing two sets of costs: the costs arising from the overall stock levels of decentralized stores as opposed to the extra handling costs involved with central storage.

For an individual commodity, the following terms are defined:

P = Purchase price per unit,

Q = *Average* demand per week in units of an individual store,

L = Lead-time (in weeks), i.e. the average time elapsing between the issue of an order and receipt of the goods,

n = Number of subsidiary stores in the region,

C_1 = Stock-holding cost per week (assumed to be the same whether at the unit or the central store),

C_2 = Transport and handling cost per item between central and unit store.

If the variations in demand follow a similar pattern to that assumed earlier, then each store can be mathematically shown to need a stock reserve of $K\sqrt{(LQ)}$ where K is a constant depending on the desired level of protection against stock running out. For a 99 per cent level of protection the value of K would be 2·33; for 97·5 per cent level the value of K would be 1·96 and so on. Note that the reserve varies according to the square-root of the expected demand in the lead-time. A fourfold increase in the demand rate only leads to a doubling of the stock reserve. Since there are n individual stores, the total safety stock-holding is therefore $nK\sqrt{(LQ)}$. If, however, the stock of the n stores is combined, the reserve required to give the same protection will be $K\sqrt{(nLQ)}$ since the expected demand in the lead-time is now nLQ when all n stores are centralized into one store. The saving in stock due to the centralizing of the stocks into a single depot will therefore be

$$nK\sqrt{(LQ)} - K\sqrt{(nLQ)}$$

or

$$K\sqrt{(nLQ)}(\sqrt{n} - 1)$$

Since the stock-holding cost is C_1 per item, the total money saving per week through central storage will be

$$C_1 \times K\sqrt{(nLQ)}(\sqrt{n} - 1)$$

But extra transport and handling costs are involved in getting the stocks from the central store to the individual store locations, and these costs must be set against the savings from the reduced level of safety stocks held. The total demand from the n stores is nQ per week, and since the transport and handling costs are C_2, it follows that the total cost of handling goods from a central depot is nQC_2.

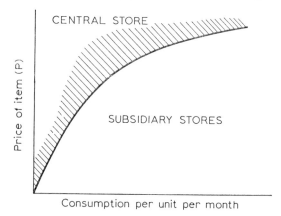

Figure 7.5b Centralized store system

Clearly, it will pay to store goods centrally if, and only if, the extra handling costs are less than the savings, that is to say, if

$$nQC_2 < C_1 K \sqrt{(nLQ)} \, (\sqrt{n} - 1)$$

or

$$Q < \frac{1}{n} \frac{C_1{}^2 K^2 L}{C_2{}^2} (\sqrt{n} - 1)^2$$

(The symbol $<$ means "is less than.")

Given the cost of holding stock (C_1), the handling and transport costs (C_2), the number of stores (n), and the lead-time (L), the formula gives the level of weekly demand at which it is economic to consider central storage. This condition can be demonstrated graphically, as shown in Figure 7.5(*b*). The position of an item on the figure is set by its price (proportional to C_1) and consumption. If the item falls in the shaded portion, then it is worthwhile storing the item centrally. If the item is below the line, then decentralized storage should be retained.

7.8 Industrial Dynamics

Simulation can be a very valuable tool in the study of inventory and the corresponding production systems. One notable contributor in this field has been the American professor, J. W. Forrester, who has considered the dynamics of a production/distribution system in some detail and, in particular, the effect that changes have on such systems. Figure 7.6 illustrates one of his studies relating to a production/distribution system for durable consumer goods with inventories at factory, wholesalers, and retailers. For this study, the time-lag between retail sales and the arrival of replacement orders at the factory via the wholesaler's office is eight weeks. A further six weeks' delay occurs before factory output can be adjusted to respond to changes in demand. It is assumed that the various stages in the system aim to keep a fixed number of weeks' supply in stock and that the inventory held is therefore adjusted from time to time in line with changes in demand made by the next lower unit in the system. A computer simulation is then used to show the effect of changes on this otherwise stable system. The figure shows the effects following an immediate and once-and-for-all sustained rise of 10 per cent in retail demand from January. The balance of the system is upset to a frightening degree. Because the factory is late in adjusting to the increase, output has to rise abnormally and reaches about +40 per cent in May. This rise is, of course, an overswing and there is a subsequent drop back to a level 3 per cent below the original (or 13 per cent below the revised) demand rate. Inventories similarly go up and down like a yo-yo. If, instead of a once-and-for-all rise of 10 per cent, the demand were subject to seasonal fluctuations of ±10 per cent, the resulting effects on the level of production demonstrate even more marked variations, which persist a good deal longer than previously.

Effects such as those being simulated here can be observed from time to time in much of British industry, particularly in the heavy sector of industry. Steel works are heard of operating at only 60 per cent of the normal rate at a time when the consumption of steel in the economy is only 5 per cent or 10 per cent down. It is those production units which are at the end of a long chain of processes that are most exposed to this kind of apparently erratic variation. Analyses such as Forrester's can do a lot to assist in diagnosing the problems and thus helping to formulate methods which will soften the impact and the loss of efficiency that would otherwise be concomitant with such fluctuations.

Individual company positions can be simulated in a similar manner. For example, a tyre firm was concerned about the sharp rises and falls in its cash and inventory balances over the year. Problems of repeatedly running out of stock and then building up excessive stocks were hampering the company's operations, and management began to question the methods being used to order new stock. Basically

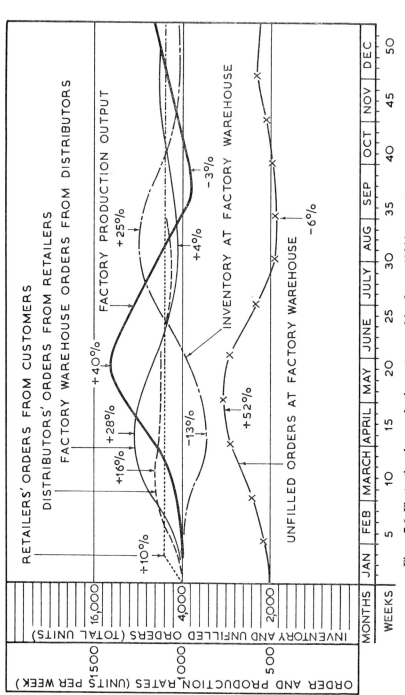

Figure 7.6 Fluctuations in a production system resulting from a 10% increase in demand

the rule used was to have enough stock on hand to satisfy the sales demand for two months. Two months' sales demand was determined by adding up sales of the past thirteen weeks and multiplying by two-thirds. The number of tyres to be ordered was then found by subtracting the actual number of tyres in the inventory from this figure. The trouble seems to have occurred, not from bad delivery records, but from seasonal business. For example, peaks commonly occur in October and April, whilst sales decline sharply in January and July. These peaks and troughs are frequently around 40 per cent of the normal demand level. The construction of a general simulation model of the situation enables the following questions, amongst others, to be studied:

(a) The effects of an ordering rule which recognizes the seasonal pattern of demand,
(b) The effect of responding more slowly (or more quickly) to changes in sales pattern as far as ordering more or less in inventory is concerned,
(c) The effect of reducing the time lag between the time the product is ordered and the time it is delivered.

By setting up a series of mathematical equations the appropriate study can be made and alternative policies examined on paper without the need to try out each alternative in practice.

7.9 Inventory Control Systems

The simple type of stock control system described earlier is defined by two quantities. The first defines the stock level below which a new order is to be placed, the other gives the quantity then to be ordered. Such a system can be operated through what is referred to as the two-bin system. Under this system the units of stock, say steel rods, are held in two bins 1 and 2. Stock is taken from bin 1 as required until this bin is empty. More rods are then ordered, the amount being determined from the standard formula (v) given on page 94. Meanwhile, until delivery occurs, stock is used from bin 2. The standard amount in bin 2 is calculated to be the expected demand in the lead-time plus the safety stock. When the replenishments arrive, bin 2 is filled up to its quota and the rest is placed in bin 1. The procedure is then repeated. If demand were changing, the amount ordered would vary and forecast changes in demand could be similarly allowed for.

An alternative system is the constant cycle system under which orders are placed at a constant interval of time, rather than at a fixed level of stock held. This time interval will often be chosen for administrative convenience, although it should properly be found by a minimum-cost procedure as outlined in earlier sections. The quantity ordered each time will be enough to meet the sales forecast for the next interval (adjusted for stock held, lead-time, demand, and safety stock). This system is especially advantageous when it is desired to co-ordinate the orders for several items from the same source.

For a stable situation (demand steady, lead-time constant, costs fixed) the two systems will generally be equally effective. If some of these factors are varying, differences may arise. The two-bin system responds to such changes by altering both the re-order quantity and the interval between orders. The constant cycle system can only change its re-order quantity and consequently needs to do so to a rather greater degree. This is reflected in the rather greater fluctuation in stock levels commonly observed under such conditions in the constant cycle system, in turn leading to a higher average stock. The constant cycle system loses some of its sluggishness if it is designed not only to meet expected demand, but also to apply a stock correction which depends on the difference between the measured stock and a target stock. Such systems can, however, become very unstable and give freak results in certain conditions, leading to a lack of confidence.

7.10 Feedback Control Systems

Any inventory control system needs to be of a feedback dynamic nature, able to take advantage of changing circumstances as quickly as is feasible. Such a feedback system aims to take account of past information from the system to make new rules for obtaining more effective control in the future. This may involve amending from time to time the order-quantity or lead-time or safety stock. Figure 7.7 shows schematically what is meant by such a control system. The physical operations of the system, concerned with say the steel held by a stock-holder, lead to replenishments of stock and demands being made on it. The decision as to when and how much stock to replenish is gauged by the re-order level and the re-order quantity which will have been fixed by reference to the target level of investment and/or protection set by the management. The performance and financial data thrown up will be compared with the targets which were also set by the management. The re-order level (ROL) and re-order quantity (ROQ) will also be critically dependent upon the forecasting system used for the scheme, and the righthand side of the figure is designed to show how the forecasting system itself both feeds into the re-ordering system and needs to be monitored. It

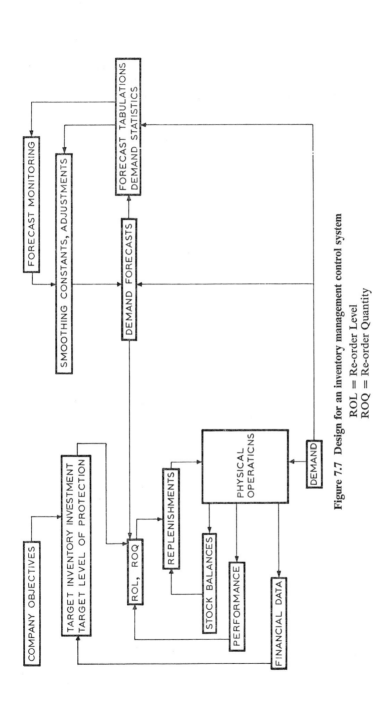

Figure 7.7 Design for an inventory management control system

ROL = Re-order Level

ROQ = Re-order Quantity

may be of a simple form, say the so-called exponential forecasting system, where the new forecast s_1 is related to the previous forecast s_0 and actual demand s by a relation of the type

$$s_1 = s_0 + \alpha(s - s_0)$$

with α as a "smoothing" constant. The value of α will then need to be monitored and possibly adjusted from time to time. (For a fuller discussion of these forecasting techniques, see reference 4 by Brown and 7 by Trigg at end of chapter.)

Exponential forecasting is a specific example of a feedback control

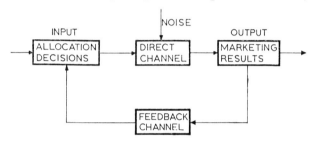

Figure 7.8 Feedback control system

system which is shown in skeleton form in Figure 7.8. Basically there is an input, some random disturbances (commonly referred to as noise) affecting the assumptions originally made concerning the events generating the system, and then an output, possibly of marketing results. As a consequence of these effects, some feedback control is necessary to control the allocation decisions which are being made. It is a continuing loop and the objective of the system is to maximize the function concerned (profit, protection, etc.) on a long-term basis in such a manner that changes in the pattern, say of demand or deliveries, are catered for automatically.

REFERENCES

(1) *Introduction to Operations Research* by C. W. Churchman *et al.* (Wiley, 1957) (Chapters 8 to 10).
(2) *Production Planning and Inventory Control* by J. F. Magee (McGraw-Hill).
(3) *A Guide to Stock Control* by A. Battersby (Pitman, 1962).
(4) *Decision Rules for Inventory Management* by R. G. Brown (Holt, Rinehart and Winston).
(5) *Scientific Inventory Control* by W. E. Welch (Management Publishing Corporation).
(6) *Industrial Dynamics* by J. W. Forrester (M.I.T.).
(7) Monitoring a forecast system, by D. W. Trigg, *Operational Research Quarterly* (1964), Vol. 15, pp. 271–274.

8 Decision Analysis

8.1 Introduction

Decision-making contains both psychological and rational factors. For a "satisfactory" decision, the two factors must be consistent. Decision theory studies the *rational* factor in order to clarify the situation and so increase the chance of attaining consistency. It does not make the final decision for the manager—the manager himself is paid to do that, and his ultimate success depends upon his ability to judge correctly the right blend of psychological and rational factors.

The elements involved in decision-making under conditions of uncertainty are:

(*a*) A number of possible *actions*, one of which is to be selected, but all of which are affected by

(*b*) A number of *states* of nature, or outcomes dependent upon a set of uncertain external factors, any one of which may hold, and each of which can affect

(*c*) The *value* or consequence, to the decision-maker, of taking any of the available actions in the light of the possible states of nature, and

(*d*) The *criteria* by which the decision-maker judges between alternatives.

These data can be conveniently presented in the form of a pay-off matrix. As a simple illustration, consider a problem concerning the weather and a swimming pool. Suppose that a ticket allowing the bearer to use a swimming pool all week-end costs 7 m.u.* if purchased during the preceding week, but a single day's admission costs 5 m.u. if paid on the day itself. Your alternative actions are, therefore, to buy a week-end ticket or to buy daily tickets. You intend to go swimming whenever the weather is fine, but not otherwise. During the week-end there can be 0, 1 or 2 fine days and these outcomes

---

* All monetary units in this chapter are expressed as m.u. so as to make the arguments used independent of the particular currency concerned. The symbol m.u. will be dropped unless required for clarity.

are denoted by b_1, b_2 and b_3. These are the three possible outcomes that can arise. Then the pay-off matrix displaying the values of each action/outcome combinations would take the following form:

			State (event)			
			b_1	b_2	b_3	
			0	1	2	fine days
Action	a_1	Week-end ticket	−7	−7	−7	
	a_2	Daily ticket	0	−5	−10	

The figures in the table represent the amount paid out for each action against the various outcomes. Under a_1 the cost is always 7; under a_2, it can be 0, 5 or 10. A negative sign is inserted since the quantities tabulated are paid out. Some procedure is now needed to guide choice amongst the possible actions.

8.2 Maximin Decision Rule

Suppose you hold a pessimistic view of life and it is assumed that whatever action is taken, nature will arrange the weather to your maximum pecuniary disadvantage. The safest action might be to take such a course as will make the best of a bad job, i.e. to take that action for which the maximum possible cost is least. This leads to the so-called maximin decision rule.

Applied to the swimming ticket problem the steps would be to take the minimum (or worst) pay-off for each action and then to select the action whose minimum is the maximum (i.e. the best amongst the minima).

Action	*Minimum pay-off for this action*	*Maximum of these minima*
a_1	−7	−7
a_2	−10	

Hence action a_1 should be selected and a week-end ticket bought. By this action the maximum possible expenditure is limited to 7; with the other allowable action the possible expenditure could have been as high as 10. This rule is simple and straightforward, leading to an unequivocal solution, but it has certain snags.

To illustrate one of the major snags, consider a different problem when the rule is used in order to decide whether or not to undertake some research work. The two possible actions are either that the research is undertaken, or that it is not. The two possible states (or outcomes) are that a cash return of X is achieved for an expenditure of C, or alternatively that C is expended with no return. The appropriate pay-off matrix will be as follows:

	State (event)			
	b_1 Research succeeds	b_2 Research fails	Minimum of row	Maximum of row minima
Action a_1 Do research	$X - C$	$-C$	$-C$	
a_2 Don't do research	0	0	0	0

Hence the decision under the maximin rule would be a_2 or "don't do research." Indeed, whatever the value of X, the answer would be the same and no research would be done. This is frankly unreasonable, and so the maximin rule cannot be adopted as a universal method of decision appraisal.

8.3 Minimax Regret Rule

It is obvious that in most practical problems, it is too pessimistic to assume that the worst will always happen. If such an attitude were adopted, the decision-maker would look with regret at lost opportunities. What is meant by regret in this connection? The regret for any action/outcome combination is defined as the difference between (a) the maximum possible pay-off under that outcome and (b) the pay-off resulting from the action/outcome combination concerned, i.e. it is the amount of pay-off lost by not taking the optimal action for the (subsequently known) outcome concerned. Thus in the swimming pool problem, under the combination a_1/b_1, the pay-off is -7. On the other hand, if outcome b_1 did in fact occur but action a_2 had been taken, the pay-off would be 0. Hence the subsequent regret at choosing a_1 rather than a_2 is $0 - (-7)$ or 7. A table (or matrix) can now be written in which all the entries are not pay-offs as before, but regrets as calculated above. The table will run as follows:

		Outcome b_1	b_2	b_3	Maximum of row	Minimum of maxima
Action	a_1	7	2	0	7	
	a_2	0	0	3	3	3

To select the best action the maximum (greatest) regret is tabulated for each action and that action chosen for which the maximum regret is a minimum (least). Under this rule, therefore, action a_2 to buy daily tickets would be selected, on the grounds that this minimizes the maximum possible regret.

How does this principle look when applied to the R & D matrix of the previous section? The appropriate regret matrix will be

		Outcome b_1	b_2	Maximum of row	Minimum of maxima
Action	a_1	0	C	C	?
	a_2	$X - C$	0	$X - C$	?

(It is assumed, reasonably, that X is greater than C, i.e. that the successful outcome would more than cover the research cost.)

Action a_1, do research, would be selected if $X - C$ is greater than C, which is equivalent to X being greater than $2C$. Otherwise action a_2, don't do research, would be selected. This result is not uncommonly quoted as a rule of thumb in research management, namely carry out an R & D project if the gross return from a successful outcome is at least twice the cost, otherwise drop it.

Having derived rationally such a rule of thumb, suppose that an inventor approached your firm and offered to develop a perpetual motion machine for £1m. Success would certainly be worth more than £2 m. so that under the rule, you should accept the offer. But would you do so? You would be very unlikely to accept, however, because although the rule is satisfied, there is a crucial missing element, namely your belief in the feasibility of the proposal. This degree of belief must, in practice, colour the decision you make and needs therefore to be brought into the assessment. To illustrate this, a further example will be analysed.

8.4 Installation of a Boiler

Suppose you have to decide upon the best type of boiler to install in a large factory. (This problem is based on a 1963 situation.) Basically, three alternatives are open to you:

(*a*) to install a coal-fired boiler,
(*b*) to install an oil-fired boiler,
(*c*) to install a dual-fired boiler capable of conversion from one fuel to the other at a negligible extra cost.

Table 8.1 gives the capital and annual running costs, as at the appropriate date, for the three types of boiler.

TABLE 8.1

Alternative Boiler Costs

	Boiler type		
	I Coal only (a_1)	II Oil only (a_2)	III Dual-fired both fuels (a_3)
Capital cost	1·95	1·50	2·40
Annual running cost	0·90	0·90	0·90

(All figures in 1,000 m.u.)

Although the fuels would lead to identical running costs at present costs, the long-term fuel price position might be rather different. After taking advice, you decide that it is reasonable to assume that the price differential, on a heat equivalent basis, which could possibly arise will range from coal being $12\frac{1}{2}$ per cent higher than oil to oil being $12\frac{1}{2}$ per cent higher than coal. Hence the three extreme outcomes to be considered are set at

b_1 Coal $12\frac{1}{2}$ per cent up
b_2 Prices equal
b_3 Oil $12\frac{1}{2}$ per cent up

You also decide that the period to be considered is 25 years and that the appropriate interest factor to apply to the capital invested is 15 per cent. The pay-off matrix has first to be calculated. The capital involved for each action is amortised (written off) at 15 per cent over 25 years to convert the single capital payment into a corresponding, but alternative, annual payment. (See, for example, *Capital Budgeting and Company Finance*, by A. J. Merrett and A. Sykes, for a description of the discounting technique involved in such a calculation.) These annual values for the three types of boiler are

a_1: 0·3016 a_2: 0·2320 a_3: 0·3712

The pay-off matrix can now be calculated on an annual basis. It is assumed that the cheaper fuel remains at 0·9 annual cost, the alternative rising by $12\frac{1}{2}$ per cent or $12.5 \times 0.9/100 = 0.1125$. The basic cost of 0·9 can be imputed as an extra addition to all the

TABLE 8.2

Matrix of Pay-offs

		Outcome b_1	b_2	b_3	Minimum of row	Maximum of row minima
	a_1	−1·3141	−1·2016	−1·2016	−1·3141	
Action	a_2	−1·1320	−1·1320	−1·2445	−1·2445	−1·2445
	a_3	−1·2712	−1·2712	−1·2712	−1·2712	

possible combinations of action/outcome. Table 8.2 gives the combined costs for each action/outcome combination. For example, the action/outcome combination a_1/b_1 costs 0·3016 for capital and 0·9 + 0·1125 for running costs, 1·3141 in all. Under the maximin procedure the optimum decision would be to install an oil-fired boiler, since this will maximize the minimum possible pay-offs for each alternative action.

Suppose now that the minimax regret rule were considered in place of the maximin rule. Table 8.3 then gives the regrets for the various actions, derived from the appropriate pay-offs in Table 8.2. Thus under outcome b_1, the best action is a_2; hence the regret for combination a_2/b_1 is zero. For combination a_1/b_1 it will accordingly be −1·1320 − (−1·3141) = 0·1821, etc.

The maximum regret is now found for each action and the action for which the maximum is a minimum located. Once again the same conclusion would be reached, namely to install an oil boiler. It can be seen, however, that the action deduced begs the question as to the likelihood of the various outcomes arising. The degree of belief in the various outcomes should be brought in, since they may be considered to have very different likelihood of occurrence, and this in turn could affect the desirability of the various actions. For

TABLE 8.3

Matrix of Regrets

		Outcome b_1	b_2	b_3	Maximum of row	Minimum of row maxima
	a_1	0·1821	0·0696	0	0·1821	
Action	a_2	0	0	0·0429	0·0429	0·0429
	a_3	0·1392	0·1392	0·0696	0·1392	

instance, if it were thought that b_3 was the virtually certain outcome in practice, then action a_1, installing the coal boiler, should be followed.

8.5 Expected Values

Return now to the R & D illustration of sections 8.2 and 8.3 and assume that you have the choice between either being allowed to have the option of making the decision on the R & D project or alternatively taking part in a lottery. This lottery consists of 100 similar tickets in a big drum. The only difference between the tickets is that some are marked "win" and the rest are marked "lose." You are given the straight choice:

either   to gamble on the success of the research

or   to draw one ticket at random from the drum, the writing on that ticket deciding the outcome of the research.

In each case the possible monetary outcome if the gamble succeeds is the same. How many winning tickets would you require there to be in the drum amongst the tickets if you are to be indifferent as to which choice to accept? Note that if none of the tickets were marked "win" you would prefer to gamble on the research, as there is presumably some finite chance of research success. Similarly, if all 100 tickets are marked "win" you would prefer the lottery, as there is some finite chance of the research failing and taking part in the lottery would give you a defined monetary profit. Hence there must be some changeover point between these two extremes.

For example, you might feel you were indifferent between a gamble on whether to go ahead with the research and a gamble in which you drew a single ticket from the 100 in the drum, of which 70 are marked "win." The probability of drawing a winning ticket is obviously 0·7, and this figure is therefore applied to your degree of belief that the research will succeed. It follows that your belief that the research will not succeed is measured by $1 - 0·7$, or 0·3. These "subjective probabilities" are referred to as *a priori* probabilities and were first suggested by Thomas Bayes (an 18th century Englishman who had in the circumstances the rather unexpected occupation of clergyman). The suggested decision procedure is then to calculate a *weighted average* of the outcome of each action, the weights being the *a priori* probabilities attached to each outcome. The action showing the maximum weighted average is then selected as the best action to take.

If this principle is applied to the R & D pay-off matrix with the *a priori* probability of success of 0·7, this gives:

	Outcome		Weighted average
Weights	b_1 0·7	b_2 0·3	
Action a_1	$X - C$	$-C$	$0·7(X - C) - 0·3C = 0·7X - C$
Action a_2	0	0	$0·7(0) + 0·3(0) = 0$

Hence action a_1 would be best provided $0·7X - C$ were greater than 0, i.e. provided X were greater than $\frac{1·0}{7}C$; otherwise action a_2 should be carried out.

In the case of the perpetual motion project you would probably visualize the drum with a million or more tickets, only one of which would read "win." Hence X would need to be very large indeed for the project to be tempting; indeed, if there were just one winning ticket amongst a million tickets, X would have to exceed $1,000,000C$ for the project to appear acceptable.

8.6   Concept of Repeatability

Note that this translation to expected (or weighted) values introduces a new concept—the concept of repeatability or a sequence of decisions. For any one single decision the outcome will be one from the set of possible outcomes; for the research problem the set consists of $X - C$ or 0. Hence expected value is meaningless when compared to that individual decision in isolation by itself; the action leads to the pay-off corresponding to one or other of the outcomes, not to some mixture of them. If the right choice is made there will be a high pay-off; if the wrong choice is made there will be a low pay-off. The expected value itself cannot and will not in general be precisely achieved, the actual results being sometimes better and sometimes worse than the expected value. But what is true is that if a large number of individual projects are each judged in this way and the appropriate decisions made, the total gain from all projects combined will approximate to the total of the individual project expected values.

This effect can be seen by considering Figure 8.1. The figure relates to the accuracy of forecasting the return on capital investments for a sample of 100 large projects carried out in a big United Kingdom company over a ten-year period. The average cost per project exceeded £$\frac{1}{2}$ m. The comparison is between the forecast return when the projects were sanctioned and the return achieved in the first full year of operation. The degree of accuracy in forecasting has been estimated by taking the difference between the achieved return and the forecast return and expressing this as a percentage of the forecast return. Put formally

Inaccuracy of forecast (%)

$$= \frac{\text{Achieved return - Forecast return}}{\text{Forecast return}} \times 100$$

A positive result means that the achieved return was greater than the forecast return, and a negative answer shows that the achieved

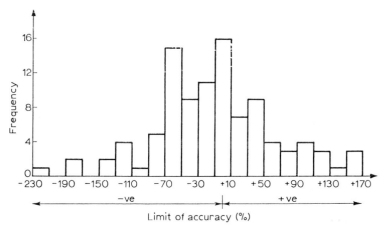

Figure 8.1 Inaccuracy of forecasting

return failed to come up to the forecast figure. The results obtained on the 100 projects ranged from −220 per cent to +169 per cent (Figure 8.1). The overall average accuracy showed that the actual return was less than forecast, by some 9·6 per cent of the forecast. But it is interesting and revealing that, whilst the 100 projects individually showed such wide variations in achieved return, the average was so close to the expected overall average of zero. Bearing in mind, however, that the forecast return for any individual project must essentially be a weighted average of expectations, this is perhaps not so surprising.

The data just described was from a single British company. D. S. Tull (see reference 8 at end of chapter) describes a similar kind of exercise carried out on 63 projects drawn from 16 different companies with very similar results. In his case the criterion calculated is based on sales or profits over a five-year period, but the spread is of very much the same magnitude, namely:

Sales -99%
to $+720\%$ ($+167\%$ if one project is excluded)

Profits -800% (-134% if two projects are excluded)
to $+140\%$

The mean forecast error, ignoring the sign of the error, was 65 per cent, and in 66 per cent of the projects the actual sales fell short of the forecast sales. It seems reasonable to conclude once again that the individual errors on forecasts have a high variability, even though the average error over a large number of products may be relatively small.

For a large company the expected monetary value (EMV) method will be a good approach provided that its forecasting system has no bias. For a small company which may live or die by one single project the problem is rather more difficult and the maximin approach may be more relevant. To illustrate these forms of analysis further, an example concerning a chemical company investment situation will be examined in some detail.

8.7 The Dissolving Chemical Company

The manager of this company has to decide whether to build a small plant or a large one to manufacture a new product with an expected market life of ten years. The decision hinges partly on the size of the market the company can obtain for the product.

Demand may possibly be high during the first two years but, if many of the initial users find the products unsatisfactory, the demand could then fall to a low level thereafter. High initial demand might alternatively indicate the possibility of a sustained high-volume market. If the demand is initially high and remains so and the company finds itself with insufficient capacity within the first two years, competitive products will certainly be introduced by other manufacturers.

If the company initially builds a big plant, it must live with it for the whole ten years, whatever the size of the market demand. If it builds a small plant, there is the option of expanding the plant in two years' time, an option that it would only take up if demand were high during the introductory period. If a small plant is built initially and demand is low during the introductory period, the company will maintain operations in the small plant and make a good profit on the low-volume throughput.

The manager is uncertain as to the action he should take. The company grew rapidly during the early 1960s, keeping pace with the chemical industry generally. The new product, if the market turns out to be large, offers the company a chance to move into a new period of extremely profitable growth. The development department, particularly the development project engineer, is anxious to build the large-scale plant in order to exploit the first major product development the department has had in some years.

The chairman, a principal stockholder, is wary of the possibility of having a large amount of plant capacity lying idle. He favours a smaller initial plant commitment, but recognizes that possible later expansion to meet high-volume demand would, overall require more investment and be less efficient to operate. The chairman also recognizes that, unless the company moves promptly to fill the demand which develops, once the product is on the market, competitors will be tempted to move in with equivalent products.

Various items of information have been obtained, or estimated, by the appropriate managers within the company. This information is summarized as follows:

(a) Marketing information
The marketing manager suggests a 60 per cent chance of a large market in the long run and a 40 per cent chance of a low demand, developing initially as follows:

Initially high, sustained high	60%	
Initially high, long-term low	10%	Low 40%
Initially low, continuing low	30%	
Initially low, subsequently high	0%	

(b) Annual income
The management accounting section have put forward the following financial estimates:

(i) A large plant with high market volume would yield £1 m. annually in cash flow (for ten years).

(ii) A large plant with low market volume would yield only £0·1 m. annually because of high fixed costs and inefficiencies.

(iii) A small plant with low market demand would be economical and would yield annual cash income of £0·4 m. per annum.

(iv) A small plant, during an initial period of high demand, would yield £0·45 m. per annum, but this would drop to £0·25 m. per annum in the long run if high demand continued, because of competition from other manufacturers.

(v) If an initial small plant were expanded after two years to meet sustained high demand, it would yield £0·7 m. annually for the remaining eight years and so would be less efficient than a large plant built initially.

(vi) If the small plant were expanded after two years, but high demand were not sustained, the estimated annual cash flow for the remaining eight years would be £0·05 m.

(c) Capital costs
Estimates obtained from construction companies indicate that a large plant would cost £3 m. to build and put into operation, a small plant would cost £1·3 m. initially and an additional £2·2 m. if expanded after two years.

The manager must decide now upon his initial action. Should he recommend the company to build or not, and if it is to build, should it build big or small? It will be assumed that the firm uses expected monetary value (EMV) as its criterion for decision. Further, for purposes of simplicity, discounting of the cash flows will be ignored (equivalent to assuming an interest rate of zero). This does not affect the principles behind the analysis, but reduces the arithmetic enormously. The possible effects of discounting are discussed later.

8.8 The Analysis of the Problem

If no building is carried out at all, it is clear that the EMV will be zero; no expenditure, no income. Hence the problem is reduced to a consideration of the other courses of action to see whether the best of them gives an EMV which exceeds zero. As a first step, it is useful to construct a decision tree to illustrate the structure of the decision which has to be made. Figure 8.2 gives this. Each path through the tree from the start to the finish (left to right) represents a separate logical possibility. Thus the path AD represents the initial action "build big" which is then followed by the outcome of low demand for all ten years. The path AEH represents the initial action "build small," then the outcome of high demand for the first two years, followed by action to expand the plant, resulting in the outcome of low demand for the remaining eight years. Similarly for the other paths. A cursory examination of the original data will show that there would be no point in expanding a small initial plant if the demand in the first two years were low. This possibility has accordingly been omitted from path AF.

Now the power of the decision tree diagram is in the opportunity it affords for the logical analysis of the various alternatives to be studied before making a decision. Decisions, as here, are often sequential in nature and the decision tree illustrates this facet. To analyse the diagram, various quantities are required, but notice first that there are basically two decision points, labelled 1 and 2. If the decision at point 1 is to be examined, it is necessary to know the values to be placed upon the two alternatives that are then open; the value of building a small plant can be assessed only if it is known what value can be expected if decision point 2 is reached. Hence it is necessary to evaluate decision point 2 first, i.e. the diagram is

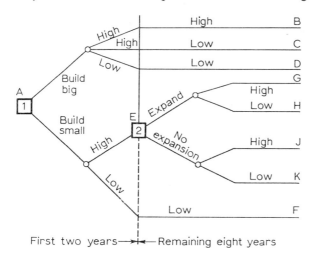

First two years—→|←—Remaining eight years

Figure 8.2 Basic decision tree

examined from right to left. This is sometimes referred to as the roll-back principle.

Decision point 2 is shown in more detail in Figure 8.3. The initial data given in section 8.7 enable the following deductions to be made for the last eight years:

$$\text{Probability of high demand} = \frac{0\cdot6}{0\cdot6 + 0\cdot1} = 0\cdot86$$

$$\text{Probability of low demand} = \frac{0\cdot1}{0\cdot6 + 0\cdot1} = 0\cdot14$$

The cash flows for the last eight years of production are entered on Figure 8.3 at the right-hand side. These are calculated from the data in section 8.7, remembering that the first two years must have given rise to high demand. Thus if the plant is expanded and there is high demand, the annual cash flow will be £0·7 m., from paragraph (*b*) (v) on page 119 in section 8.7, giving a total cash flow of 8 × 0·7, or £5·6 m. Similarly for the other possibilities.

Hence the expected monetary value (EMV) of expansion at point 2 will be:

$$\text{EMV (expansion)} = 0\cdot86 \times 5\cdot6 + 0\cdot14 \times 0\cdot4 - 2\cdot2$$
$$\phantom{\text{EMV (expansion)} = 0} \text{(high} \qquad \text{(low} \qquad \text{(capital}$$
$$\phantom{\text{EMV (expansion)} = 0} \text{demand)} \quad \text{demand)} \quad \text{cost)}$$
$$= 4\cdot82 + 0\cdot06 - 2\cdot2 = 2\cdot68$$

(Note that since 2·2 represents an outlay as opposed to a gain, it is shown as a negative gain.)

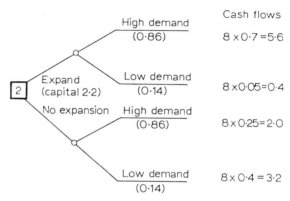

Figure 8.3 Decision at point 2
(Probabilities are shown in brackets)

Similarly, for no expansion the financial situation is:

$$\text{EMV (no expansion)} = 0\cdot86 \times 2\cdot0 + 0\cdot14 \times 3\cdot2$$
$$\phantom{\text{EMV (no expansion)} = 0} \text{(high} \qquad \text{(low}$$
$$\phantom{\text{EMV (no expansion)} = 0} \text{demand)} \quad \text{demand)}$$
$$= 1\cdot72 + 0\cdot45 = 2\cdot17$$

(Note that there is no extra capital expenditure incurred by this action.)

As the former EMV exceeds the latter (2·68 versus 2·17) the decision, if point 2 were reached, would be to expand the plant, on the grounds that expansion gives rise to a higher EMV. The expected value of the decision at that moment of time would be 2·68.

Using this analysis for decision point 2 the original decision tree can now be modified to give the tree shown in Figure 8.4. In this revised figure, decision point 2 has effectively been replaced by an expected monetary value equivalent. The complete tree can now be evaluated on similar lines to those used above. For the decision to build big, this gives:

EMV (build big)

$$= 0.6 \times 10 + 0.1 \times 2.8 + 0.3 \times 1 - 3$$

(high   (high/low   (low   (capital

demand)   demand)   demand)   cost)

$$= 6 + 0.28 + 0.3 - 3$$
$$= 3.58$$

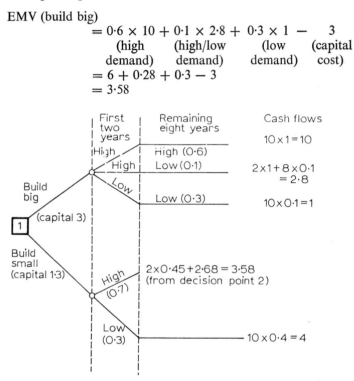

Figure 8.4 Decision at point 1
(Probabilities are shown in brackets)

Similarly, for the decision to build small:

EMV (build small)

$$= 0.7 \times 3.58 + 0.3 \times 4 - 1.3$$

(decision   (low   (capital

point 2)   demand)   cost)

$$= 2.51 + 1.2 - 1.3$$
$$= 2.41$$

Since the EMV for "build big" exceeds that for "build small" (3.58 versus 2.41) the decision would be to build big initially. The expected monetary value of such a decision would be 3.58.

This analysis has ignored, as stated at the beginning, any discounting of the cash flows. The principles of analysis would remain unaltered but the effect of an interest rate above zero would be to take account of the precise timings of the cash inflows and outflows. The overall effect would be to increase the value of the second alternative (build small) in relation to the first alternative, since some part of the capital outlay is postponed, but the magnitude of the effect would depend upon the rate of interest used in the analysis.

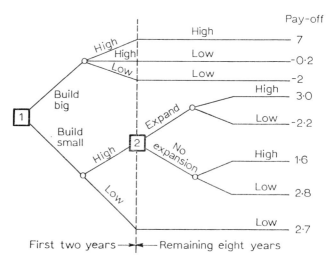

Figure 8.5 Maximin approach to decision

The analysis has been carried out using the principle of Expected Monetary Value. Therefore, although "build big" has the higher EMV there is also a non-negligible chance (0·3) of a loss of 2 occurring if this action is followed. Examining the problem under the maximin approach, Figure 8.5 gives the pay-off results for all possible decisions. Table 8.4 follows the usual approach of forming the row minima and then taking the maximum of these row minima. This table demonstrates that action a_3, namely "build small" and never expand under any circumstances, would be the maximin solution and must give a profit of at least 1·6. Any other course could lead to a loss under certain circumstances. Hence a play-safe policy gives a rather different result from EMV, but such a decision process ignores possibilities such as a gain of 7 which could occur under a "build big" action. For a small firm to whom a possible loss of 2·0 would be disastrous, the maximin approach is probably relevant;

TABLE 8.4

Pay-offs for Various Alternatives

Demand		State (outcome)			Minimum of row	Maximum of row minima
		b_1 High	b_2 High/Low	b_3 Low		
Action	a_1 (Build big)	7·0	−0·2	−2·0	−2·0	
	a_2 (Build small/ expand)	3·0	−2·2	2·7	−2·2	
	a_3 (Build small/ not expand)	1·6	2·8	2·7	1·6	1·6

for larger firms for whom the current decision is one of a series of such decisions the EMV approach would be the more relevant.

8.9 Risk Aversion

As was pointed out earlier, the risks of business decisions are often small enough to allow the decision-maker to base his analysis on expected consequences. This was so in the case of the chemical company. If, however, a substantial part of the business is at risk, an analysis which pushes aside the decision-maker's attitude to risk aversion may be seriously unsound. Fortunately, risk aversion can be incorporated quite straightforwardly into a decision tree as long as the decision-maker's general attitude towards risk can be quantified. This requires the construction of what is known as a preference or utility curve, of which an illustration is given in Figure 8.6.

A preference curve translates monetary consequences (shown as the horizontal axis) into corresponding "utility" values which typically range from zero to one. In this figure, using the top curve, a loss of £200,000 is shown to have a utility of 0·1, break-even has a utility of 0·7, and gaining £600,000 has a utility of 0·9. The effect of using a curve of this kind in order to read off utility values is to move the decision tree analysis away in the direction of risk avoidance in a precise way.

The technique of establishing a decision-maker's attitude to risk is discussed elsewhere (see reference 4 by Schlaifer at end of chapter). A usual approach is to elicit the decision-maker's attitude to a few hypothetical gambling situations, e.g. how much would he take for sure in exchange for a 50:50 chance of receiving £0 or £600,000 in his prevailing economic condition? From such assessments, a few points on the curve can be deduced and the rest of the curve drawn in. If the curve has been accurately drawn, the utility numbers can be used in place of the real monetary consequences to show the

Figure 8.6 Preference curve for decision-makers

optimum strategy in accordance with the decision-maker's attitude towards risk. Note if a straight line were used to translate monetary consequences into utilities, this would impart no more than a scaling effect to the original consequences, and replacement of the consequences by the corresponding utilities would not alter the selection of the best action.

8.10 General Considerations

Use of the decision-tree approach along the lines discussed here as a basis for decision-making is a means of making more explicit the process which must be at least intuitively present in good decision-making. Such a method allows for, and indeed encourages, the revision of the nature of the decision from time to time and the maximum use of analysis, experience, and judgment. It helps to force out into the open those differences in assumptions or standards of value that underlie differences in judgment or choice. It keeps the manager from being trapped in the formalism of a rigid procedure in which there is little room for feedback, re-definition, or interplay between analysis and decision.

If the approach adopted in this chapter seems complex, then this is only because any formal approach is bound to be so, if comparison is made with a rule-of-thumb approach. In reality, a decision tree need only be as complex as the decision itself. If the decision is a simple choice from amongst a number of straight alternatives, then the decision tree is reduced to a single-stage analysis, i.e. the use of the present value technique applied to alternative cash flows. For more complicated situations, more stages and alternatives are necessary. Explicit use of these concepts in decision analysis will help to force a consideration of alternatives, define the problems for investigation, and clarify for the manager the nature of the risks he faces and the estimates he must make. The concept can thereby contribute to the quality of those decisions which the managers and only the managers themselves must make.

REFERENCES

(1) *Elementary Decision Theory* by H. Chernoff and L. E. Moses (Chapman and Hall).
(2) *Design for Decision* by I. D. J. Bross (Macmillan).
(3) *Decision and Value Theory* by P. C. Fishburn (Wiley).
(4) *Introduction to Statistics for Business Decisions* by R. Schlaifer (McGraw-Hill).
(5) *The Compleat Strategyst* by J. D. Williams (McGraw-Hill).
(6) Decision trees for decision-making, by J. F. Magee, *Harvard Business Review*, Vol. 42, No. 4, 1964, pp. 126–138.
(7) How to use decision trees in capital investment, by J. F. Magee, *Harvard Business Review*, Vol. 42, No. 5, 1964, pp. 79–96.
(8) The relationships of actual and predicted sales and profits in new-product introductions, by D. S. Tull, *Journal of Business*, Vol. 40, No. 3, 1967, pp. 233–250.

9 Some Further Operational Research Problems

9.1 Introduction

The earlier chapters of this book have developed much of the problem-solving activities of operational research through illustrative examples. These examples have been drawn from a wide variety of situations but, for reasons of exposition, the development has centered around applications that demonstrate each technique or approach as it is introduced. In this chapter some further illustrative problems, drawn from a wide variety of fields and using a combination of techniques, will be described to widen the range of applications. The first is taken from a problem involving the integration of transport and production facilities of a brewing organization. The second relates to the effect that the adherence to certain conventional financial ratios can have on the allocation of funds between competing capital projects. The third illustration relates to the selection of advertising media so as to maximize effectiveness for a given level of outlay. The fourth illustration is taken from a marketing situation to illustrate the use of decision theory in the analysis of a pricing problem for plastics. The fifth and final problem relates to an investigation concerning the true cost involved in the checking of invoices and goods received. Necessarily, the descriptions can only be given in outline but, where possible, follow-up references are given at the end of the chapter for those desiring to delve deeper.

9.2 Location Problem

In the earlier chapters, problems concerning production and distribution have been discussed. The current problem under discussion is one linking together production and distribution in the sense that the siting of both the production units and the distribution depots was under consideration. The organization was a brewery company who had to incur some capital expenditure if the main brewery was to continue to operate efficiently. The site of the brewery was a

valuable one and there seemed to be a good case for selling the site
and building a new brewery elsewhere. The question was where and,
more generally, should there be more than one brewery?

A schematic diagram of a brewery's distribution system is shown
in Figure 9.1. Beer is manufactured in bulk in breweries and then
packed in casks (racking), kegs, or bottles. Bottling plants are

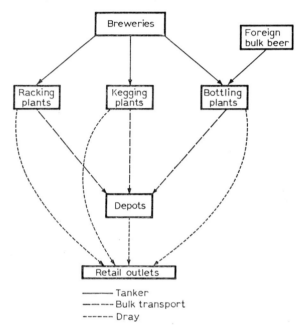

Figure 9.1 Schematic diagram of the flow of beer

frequently at separate locations from the breweries and, although
there is no technical reason why racking and kegging should not be
done at separate locations, it is unusual. The possibility that this
separation might be economic arises because of the considerably
greater transport costs by bulk transport and by dray as opposed
to tanker. So-called "foreign" beers are brewed by other companies
and sold in bulk to the present company for bottling in their own
plant. Beer in cask, keg, or bottle is transported in bulk to depots,
or by dray to individual public houses, either from the depots or
direct from the packaging plants.

To tackle this problem a considerable amount of data, falling
under four main headings, was required:

(a) *Demand forecasts*
Demand forecasts for the time during which the new system would
be expected to be operational, broken down by area and separated
into draught and bottled, in-company, and foreign beers.

(b) *Handling costs*
Handling costs separately for the depots and the racking, kegging,
and bottling plants.

(c) *Transport costs*
Transport costs for the three types of company transport in terms of
an overhead and a mileage cost.

(d) *Process costs*
The capital and operating costs for both existing and new production
plants and depots.

Obtaining this data was a relatively straightforward, but extremely
tedious, exercise. Since the accuracy and value of the final solution
depends to a considerable extent on the quality of the information
used in the analysis, time well spent at this stage was of vital importance. With the relevant data to hand, the problem was tackled
with the help of a specially written computer program designed to
describe the flow diagram shown in Figure 9.2. To use the program
it was necessary to specify the numbers of the different kinds of
facility available and their initial locations. Then the locations of
the facilities which minimized the total distribution costs were
found. The program had considerable flexibility; for example, it
was possible to fix the positions of any of the facilities and obtain
optimal locations of the remainder. One use of this was to determine
the effects on total distribution costs of retaining any existing facilities.

Nearly 100 runs were made with the computer program to gain
information using the existing site pattern, to optimize the positions
chosen, and to test the stability of the answers. These runs were
not all made together but singly or in small batches. Each set of
results was analysed to incorporate the net cost of building and
operating new facilities and closing old ones. On the basis of these
results, further computer runs were made and fresh analyses carried
out. The process can be described as interrogating the model—a
common procedure used with models of complex systems. The
recommendations that were eventually made included moving
existing bottling plants as well as two of the company's depots.

These recommendations were based on the best assumptions that
could be made about future demand and costs. Some of these
assumptions appeared to be particularly liable to error—and the

computer program was re-run to determine how they affected, not so much the distribution costs themselves, but the recommendations. Among the changes tested were

(*a*) increased utilization of the transport fleet,
(*b*) increased depot handling costs,
(*c*) changes in the assumed manning of company vehicles.

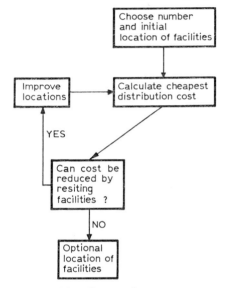

Figure 9.2 **Flow diagram of computer program**

In the first two cases, there was no effect on the recommendations, but in the third case the recommendation on depot locations was changed.

The model was also used to test out the effects of possible future acquisitions of small breweries on the optimal locations of plants and depots. A brewery takeover is made, not only for the plant and buildings, but also for the outlets, particularly the tied licensed premises. Indeed, the latter may be the prime reason for the take-over. Such an acquisition affects the geographical pattern of demand and hence the optimal location of the plant and depots. Even if a company is not presently contemplating a takeover, its planning of production and distribution facilities should take into account the effects of possible future takeovers. In this sense the model was being used to test the effects on distribution costs of changes in the pattern of sales. The whole study demonstrates the interdependence of distribution with production and sales, and shows that models can be devised to take account of all these activities. This study also illustrates the powerful use of a computer model for the analysis of planning decisions.

9.3 Capital Budgeting Procedures

The investigation outlined here had its origin in a study aimed at improving capital budgeting procedures in a medium-sized engineering firm. The study is described in greater detail by D. J. Chambers (see reference 1 at end of chapter) and relates to a budgeting problem where the firm desired to satisfy each of several overlapping but distinct criteria of performance. When managers planned major internal investments in plant and equipment, they were unwilling to restrict their attention solely to the cash flows which each investment would generate. They were concerned also with the effects on quantities shown in the balance sheet, on published profits, and on various earnings-to-assets ratios. They were very conscious that alternative investment plans could have markedly different effects on these results, and they ruled out of court those plans which, although they offered attractive rates of return, would have given rise to poor published results at some point in the planning interval.

The problem which the managers posed was not, therefore, the well-known one of choosing the list of projects whose cash flows had the highest present worth or equivalent rate of return. It was a problem of maximization subject to constraints on the published financial results.

A further aspect of their problem results from the policy that a large proportion of the firm's finance should come from internal sources. At the same time it was possible to make reasonable estimates of the kinds of investment opportunities that would occur in the next few years. Financial managers considered that an important part of their skill lay in so dovetailing projects that funds would be released by some projects just as they were required for profitable investment in others. Current projects could not be considered in isolation, and managers wished to know to what extent a future opportunity cast its shadow forward to affect the optimal current allocation of investment funds.

At the risk of some over-simplification, procedures currently followed by many progressive firms in the management and allocation of disposable funds could be characterized as follows:

(a) Decisions on the firm's financing taken at a comparatively rarefied level: on debt management, on the raising of new funds, on relations with the capital markets.

(*b*) Decisions at a more mundane level: recurrent decisions on the allocation of available funds between competing projects.

The two types of decision are linked through a figure which purports to represent the cost of new funds. If many individual projects appear to offer returns greater than this, a case can be made for increasing the volume of outside financing; and if finance becomes tighter the total amount available for allocation can be reduced.

The allocation is often made in several stages. When planning budgets have been prepared to show how the "optimal" allocation affects future financial statements, the results implied for some future period may turn out to be unacceptable. In this event the "optimal" allocation will be adjusted until it yields tolerable results. The full effects on financial statements are probably worked out only for a few alternative plans.

The method used in this particular study takes account of the financial implications of all possible plans right at the start, and proceeds to investigate further only those plans whose financial implications are acceptable.

In this situation, four constraints on reported financial results were incorporated. These were constraints which managers selected as being the most important, although different versions could easily be substituted in the analysis. The four constraints were:

(*a*) Company policy dictated that, short of dire emergency, published profits should increase from year to year. In the particular case concerned, profits were required to increase by 5% each year.

(*b*) To retain the confidence of the firm's creditors, it was thought desirable to keep the ratio of current assets to current liabilities, as reported on the balance sheet, at or above a specified value. In this case the value was taken as 3.

(*c*) A third restriction applied to dividends. It was again company policy that, subject to the usual provisos, dividends should not fall below a specified value. The case concerned illustrated a policy of maintaining dividend payment at one-third of earnings after tax, although other policies have also been investigated.

(*d*) The final restriction referred to a measure of performance: the return on gross assets. This ratio was defined as earnings before tax or depreciation, expressed as a fraction of total assets minus current liabilities. In the company under discussion, this ratio was not allowed to fall below 0·15.

Other obvious constraints were also included, e.g. a restriction on the scale at which particular projects could be undertaken.

The limitations of the information conveyed by any one of these published values or ratios need hardly be emphasized. When the National Economic Development Council (an official British Government advisory body) issued recently a league table ranking firms in the British clothing industry in the order of their return on gross assets, comments in the press from firms near the bottom of the list neatly summarized the objections to return on assets as a measure of performance. A high return may mean no more than that a revaluation of assets is long overdue. But while this particular return should certainly not be used in isolation, it is likely to appear on any short list of measures of the performance either of the whole firm or of divisions within the firm. In a world of perfect information, the published return on assets could no doubt be ignored, as a veil cloaking the reality of the underlying cash flows. But where public information about the performance and prospects of firms is imperfect and scrappy, such a measure provides the market with extra evidence. In such a world it is not irrational for managers to attempt to meet conventionally accepted requirements on published financial results.

How are managers to choose between different feasible investment plans? What is to be maximized? It was agreed that the point of view to be adopted should be that of the current owners of the firm. Managers should choose the plan most advantageous to current shareholders. It followed that the criterion adopted would have to depend in some way on the dividend policy to be followed. If a firm pays no dividend, and instead reinvests all earnings, the best plan will be the one giving the firm its highest value at the horizon. But in cases such as this one, where dividends are paid and where they are related to earnings, the shareholder will be interested both in how the investment plan affects the horizon value and in the stream of dividends which he will receive in the meantime.

If management is to identify the plan most advantageous to current shareholders, it must therefore take a position on how shareholders weigh current as against future receipts. In this case a rate of 7 per cent was used to express shareholders' preferences, although it was found that the results were broadly unaffected by reasonable variations in this figure.

The analysis was carried out through a linear programming formulation which allowed managers to take account of the diverse and complicated measures, such as those mentioned above, which the market appears to use in assessing the condition and progress of the firm. Evaluation of a firm's performance is notoriously difficult, and managers are justly sceptical of any single measure of how their capital budgeting decisions contribute to overall performance. No current system can offer more than partial and provisional solutions to a firm's capital budgeting problem. But the linear programming model can at least take account of diverse financial criteria, and it can be used to evaluate the consequential financial effects that flow from trade-offs between the various criteria. In this way it handles systematically some of the complexities and interactions which managers have to weigh up. The sorts of problem which it could answer are

(a) The optimal initial allocation between projects,
(b) The effects of borrowing extra funds at any particular time,
(c) The timing of future opportunities in the sense of how they cast their shadows forward to present actions.

Examples given in the paper quoted show that the effects can be quite marked and that the use of linear programming techniques can give results which differ widely from and are possibly better than those obtained by using standard methods of investment appraisal.

9.4 Optimum Media Schedules

This section provides a brief description of some work carried out by D. M. Ellis (see reference 2 at end of chapter) on determining an optimum media schedule in terms of its response to an advertising campaign. A sum of money £E is available to spend on an advertising campaign designed to evoke a response from a certain section of the population, and some k different media may be included in the campaign. Certain information has been made available and some assumptions have been made:

(a) *Information*
  (i) The cost of a single insertion of the type of advertisement intended in each medium. Adjustments may have to be made to deal with varying costs, discounts, etc.
  (ii) The effect of exposure is known, i.e. the probability that a person reads the issue in which an insertion appears, notices the advertisement, and is sufficiently impressed to respond. This probability will differ from person to person, i.e. a distribution of personal probability values is assumed to exist.

(b) *Assumptions*
  (i) The cost of each insertion in each medium can be specified before construction of the schedule.
  (ii) The effect of an individual exposure is not altered with the

passage of time, nor by the previous history of a person's response to the campaign.

(iii) The basic response to an advertisement for all members of the target population, and for each medium, is independent as between one person and another.

(iv) The effects of advertising in different media are independent.

A mathematical model can now be formulated to estimate the average response to various media combinations, bearing in mind that a model based on such assumptions is obviously a considerable simplification of the complicated business of advertising. The assumption about costs is not a serious restriction. Its main implication is that the format, size, and colour of insertions must be decided before beginning the optimization. This is primarily a creative decision, to be made before the media planner gets to work. For exposure values there are two elements: the probability of reading the issue concerned and the probability, having read it, of being affected by the advertisement. The former is accurately known, but only limited data are available on this second aspect, although considerable field-work is going on. Until more data become available, there is little value in discussing the effect of the assumption.

The most serious assumption, however, is that concerning the independence of exposure values. A lot of data are available on the "readership" of different media and this is the basis of the work. To be able to assume independence is desirable for two reasons. First, it gives a model which is amenable to analysis, though not too divergent from reality. Secondly, although readership data are plentiful, even these are insufficient to give accurate estimates of joint readership in some cases.

The IPA/NRS survey uses 15,000 to 17,000 interviews per year. For the twelve months to December 1965, a sample of roughly 7,200 male readers gave readership for the *Daily Mirror*, *Daily Express*, and *Daily Telegraph* of 42, 35, and 9 per cent respectively. On the independence assumption: the number of persons reading all three would be, on average, 95, and sampling variations on such a number would be quite high (see Appendix B). A few errors such as this will, however, probably have little effect in a schedule involving a reasonable number of media. But if the data are further split by status, etc., direct estimates may well be inaccurate, unless based on prohibitive amounts of data. In the face of such difficulties, simulation is often used. (See, for example, the article by E. M. L. Beale, reference 3 at end of chapter.) This has the advantage that all the complexities of the situation can, in theory, be incorporated. Against this, no computer program has yet been prepared which leads automatically to optimum schedules. At best, such a program simulates response to given schedules and perhaps evaluates minor alterations which might improve them. The information available on certain of the points mentioned above hardly justifies a high level of sophistication. Hence the two approaches may be profitably combined. The model, and the method of optimization used with it, can indicate an optimum and the way in which the optimum response increases with cost. A simulation programme can then be used to

TABLE 9.1

Short List of Media

Medium	Cost of insertion (£)	Readership amongst sample (%)	Conditional exposure value
Daily Mirror	3,225	41	0·50
Daily Express	3,000	34	0·40
Daily Mail	2,480	17	0·40
Daily Telegraph	1,930	9	0·45
News of the World	4,224	44	0·30
People	3,750	41	0·30
Sunday Express	3,750	27	0·30
Sunday Times (Colour)	2,277	9	0·45
ITV Publications	3,003	35	0·40
Radio Times	3,600	33	0·50

estimate the average response more accurately and to cast around for slight changes in the schedule which improve the response. The following example illustrates the kind of results obtained from such an approach.

Suppose that the sum of £80,000 is available for a campaign directed at men only. Table 9.1 shows the relevant data, and a simplified model is used whereby the exposure value depends on two factors:

(a) The percentage readership b_i of the ith medium amongst the target population; these readerships are assumed to be basically static and distributed independently of each other.
(b) The conditional exposure value v_i, which is the (conditional) probability that a person who reads the issue in which an insertion appears, notices the advertisement and responds to it.

It was decided to have at least one insertion in each medium, but a maximum of two insertions in each weekly paper. The coverage was to be maximized. The final schedule, using the type of model outlined earlier, and maximizing the effective coverage, is built up in Table 9.2. This schedule shows two insertions in each paper except the *Daily Mirror* (4 insertions), *Daily Express* (5), and *Daily Mail* (3). Examination of the table reveals, however, that approximately £16,000 spent on obtaining the last 2 per cent of effective coverage might not be thought worth the return. The schedule would then be terminated at 20 insertions, costing £65,000. At this point, the marginal gain from an extra £1,000 of advertising is approximately 0·16 per cent effective coverage; or, put alternatively, the cut-off point is being put where 1 per cent extra effective coverage is equated with £6,000 extra advertising expenditure. The situation is summarized graphically in Figure 9.3.

9.5   A Pricing Problem in Plastics

This is an abbreviated discussion of a paper by P. E. Green (see references 4 and 5 at end of chapter to Green and to Green and Tull). The company concerned, Everclear Plastics in the United States, had sales in excess of $300 m. in 1959 and one of its major products was Kromel plastic, selling at $1 a pound. Total demand was, however, fairly stagnant and some increase in the total capacity of the Kromel industry was expected.

Kromel plastic had been developed by Everclear in the early 1950s and was basically a modification of an older and much more widely used plastic named Verlon. Kromel was superior to Verlon in several respects, but was somewhat higher-priced. The price spread between the two had been reduced gradually, however, and in 1960 Kromel prices were only about 10 per cent above those of Verlon.

Both Kromel and Verlon plastics were sold to textile manufacturers who, in turn, sold upholstery materials to industrial users. These industrial users were classified into four major market segments:

Segment "A"   Car manufacturers, for use as original equipment (OEM) in cars.

Segment "B"   Lorry manufacturers, for use as OEM in lorries and buses.

Segment "C"   Seat cover manufacturers, for use in replacement of seat covers.

Segment "D"   Miscellaneous users, including manufacturers of aircraft, boats, etc.

TABLE 9.2

Construction of Optimum Insertion Schedule

Total insertions	Medium	Cumulated cost (£)	Effective coverage (%)
10	1 insertion each	31,239	70·4
11	*Daily Mirror*	34,464	74·2
12	*ITV Publications*	37,467	76·7
13	*Daily Express*	40,467	78·9
14	*Radio Times*	44,067	81·0
15	*People*	47,817	82·9
16	*News of the World*	52,041	84·7
17	*Daily Mirror*	55,266	85·8
18	*Daily Express*	58,266	86·7
19	*Daily Mail*	60,746	87·3
20	*Sunday Express*	64,496	88·1
21	*Daily Express*	67,496	88·6
22	*Daily Mirror*	70,721	89·0
23	*Daily Telegraph*	72,651	89·3
24	*Daily Mail*	75,131	89·6
25	*Sunday Times* (Colour)	77,408	89·8
26	*Daily Express*	80,408	90·1

(Note that each line is incremental to the previous line, i.e. assumes that all insertions up to and including that line are made.)

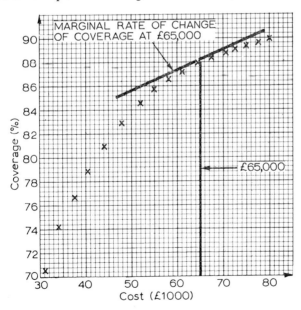

Figure 9.3 Advertising costs and marginal coverage

139

By far the most important market segment was the OEM car market, which represented about two-thirds of the total potential volume.

During the late 1950s, the superior performance characteristics of Kromel had enabled it to displace Verlon to a large extent in all market segments except car manufacture. Because of its continued dominance in this segment, total Verlon sales were more than double those of Kromel in 1959.

Everclear sales executives were sure that if the OEM car market could be penetrated by Kromel, demand in the other three segments would increase substantially as a result. This was because, to some extent, upholstery was produced and carried in stock to meet combined requirements for two or more end uses. Because of the interdependence of the other market segments with the OEM car segment, penetration of this market was regarded by Everclear management as the key to expanding the total market.

Everclear was the largest seller of Kromel with a market share in 1959 of about 40 per cent. The three competing sellers were all large companies, and it was virtually certain that any price reduction made by Everclear would be matched immediately by all competitors. Lower Kromel prices might not, however, lead to retaliation by Verlon manufacturers, since margins in the latter industry were already very low. Kromel fibre was highly standardized and all four sellers offered virtually identical product quality, technical assistance, and terms of sale.

At the outset, the manager responsible believed that it was essential to have agreement on the company objectives involved in the pricing decision, what alternatives were available to management, and the period of time to be used in the analysis. Detailed internal discussions on these points took place.

(a) Objectives

The basic objective set by the top management of Everclear for all divisions and products was to maintain a rate of return on investment of at least 20 per cent before tax. The pricing decision on Kromel could affect this objective in two ways. First, a lower price might enable sufficient expansion of sales to be achieved to offset the lower profit per unit. Secondly, a lower Kromel price might discourage the development of over-capacity in the industry and permit Everclear to maintain or even increase its share of total Kromel sales.

No additional investment in production facilities for the product was planned, since a substantially higher level of output could be handled with present space and equipment. Hence, the criterion used for comparing alternative prices was total dollar profits.

In discussing the possible effects of a price reduction, the question of the timing of the profits had to be considered. A reduction in Kromel prices would undoubtedly lead to lower profits at least for a year or two, as the market would not respond immediately. No standard rate of "interest" for compounding these profits had been adopted at Everclear, since the comparison of policy alternatives in these terms was not a regular procedure. After discussion it was suggested that the analysis be made using both a 6 per cent "interest" rate and a 10 per cent rate. The results could then be compared to see if the interest rate made any difference.

(b) Alternatives
The basic question to be answered by the study was whether a price reduction should be made on Kromel. The possibility of increasing the price was ruled out immediately, since it was regarded as virtually impossible that competing sellers would follow suit if this were done. To keep the analysis within bounds, it was desirable to consider only a limited number of alternative prices.

The lower limit of price alternatives was the variable cost per pound. The Marketing Manager felt that the lowest price worth consideration was somewhat above variable cost; he suggested 80 cents per pound as the minimum. Between the minimum of 80 cents and the *status quo* of $1, it was decided to consider two other alternatives, namely 85 cents and 93 cents per pound.

(c) Planning period
It was recognized that the effects of any decision reached on prices would be felt over at least several years in the future. Theoretically, the analysis could be made so as to cover an indefinite ("infinite") period, but it was not believed feasible to extend estimates of market behaviour beyond a definite, fairly short time span, say five years.

The problem was now defined more explicitly as follows:

Which of the four alternative prices—80 cents, 85 cents, 93 cents, or $1—would yield the greatest total net profits after taxes (valued at the *end* of the five-year period, using either a 6 per cent or a 10 per cent discount rate) over the next five years?

In the course of the initial discussions, another important consideration came to light. Apart from any price changes made by Everclear, sales of Kromel depended on the future growth of the total Kromel–Verlon market, which in turn was determined by sales of cars, lorries, seat covers, etc. Lower Kromel prices would have a negligible effect on the total market growth. Predictions of combined Kromel–Verlon sales for the next five years had been made by the Everclear Market Research group. Since the key variable in the market was car production, these forecasts were necessarily subject to considerable error. Three separate forecasts were available—an "optimistic" one, a "pessimistic" one, and a "most probable" one. The price analysis was carried out using all three forecasts and, as in the case of the interest rate, the results were compared to see how much difference the forecast would make.

In order to analyse the problem as one of decision under conditions of risk, information was required on the possible "states of nature" affecting the results of the pricing decision; on the probabilities assigned to each state of nature by management; and on estimated profit results for Everclear at various sales volume levels. The last point caused relatively little difficulty. Examination of accounting records showed that over a rather wide volume range, the total cost of Kromel sold could be estimated within a small margin of error by a simple equation of the form:

$$\text{Cost} = \text{Fixed cost} + (\text{Variable cost} \times \text{Sales volume})$$

Determination of the relevant "states of nature" and attendant probabilities posed a somewhat harder problem. In essence, what was needed was a prediction of what *might* happen if a given price reduction were made and estimates of the *likelihood* of each possible chain of events. In some problems it might be possible to vary prices experimentally, observe the results, and (if enough trials were made) to derive estimates of probabilities for the occurrence of each result. This approach did not, however, seem feasible for the Kromel price analysis.

As a result of a number of meetings, the most important factors involved were defined as:

(*a*) Kromel penetration of the OEM car upholstery market. "Penetration" was defined as any significant amount of sales in this market segment; if some minimum level of sales could be attained, it was believed that competitive imitation among the car producers would lead to an expanding participation for Kromel.

(*b*) The pattern of growth in Kromel sales to the OEM car upholstery market, once penetration had been accomplished.

(*c*) Growth in Kromel sales to the other market segments according to whether or not the OEM car segment was penetrated.

(*d*) Possible retaliation to a price reduction on Kromel by manufacturers of Verlon.

(*e*) Possible reductions in Kromel prices by competing sellers, if Everclear did not reduce its price now.

Several possibilities existed for each of these factors and the total number of possible combinations of factors was very large. For convenience in visualizing the problem, a "tree diagram" of possible chains of events was drawn. A simplified version of this diagram is shown in Figure 9.4. Each "branch" of the "tree" represents one specific series of possible events. Thus, at Stage 1, Everclear had four price alternatives. If one of these were followed—say the

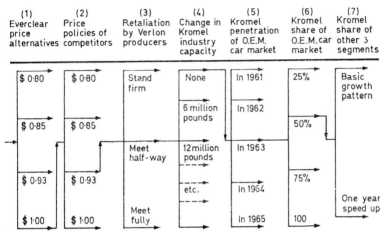

Figure 9.4 Everclear Plastics Company: simplified "tree diagram" for alternative Kromel prices

(*Note:* only a specimen set of alternatives is followed through)

standstill policy of $1—then competing sellers of Kromel might reduce their prices to any of the same (assumed) alternative levels. (If any Kromel producer lowered his price, it was assumed that all would be forced to follow suit.) For any of these possible levels of Kromel prices, Verlon producers might retaliate by meeting the reduction fully, by meeting it halfway, or by standing firm. For a given combination of Kromel and Verlon prices, penetration of the key OEM car upholstery market might be achieved by 1961, by 1962, etc. Assuming that this market segment *was* penetrated, the Kromel share of it might be as low as 25 per cent or as high as 100 per cent. Finally, for any given market share in the OEM car segment, Kromel market shares in the other three segments might follow a basic (predicted) pattern of growth or might be speeded up a year.

For each possible series of events depicted in Figure 9.4, the sales and profit consequences for Everclear were traced out. There was, in effect, another set of "branches" (not shown in Figure 9.4) corresponding to the three alternative forecasts of total Kromel–Verlon sales over the next five years. Following any one of these total forecasts and any one of the complete "chains" of Figure 9.4, a five-year forecast of Everclear's Kromel sales can be made. As previously explained, costs were estimated in relation to sales volume, so that profits on Kromel sales could be derived from the sales forecasts.

The next stage of the problem was to determine estimates of the probabilities assigned by Everclear sales personnel to each possible chain of events. In a preliminary meeting with the "outside" field sales force of five men, each salesman was asked to start thinking in terms of likely consequences of various courses of action. Following this, an all-day session was held in which the salesmen were asked to make a series of estimates of relevant probabilities for specific situations. The term "probability" was defined in the sense of "how many chances in 100 do you think there would be that a certain event would happen, given certain basic information?" Each salesman was given information on past sales of Kromel and Verlon to each market segment along with prevailing prices for each material.

The procedure for obtaining probability estimates was then as follows:

(a) Each question was stated verbally to the group.
(b) Each member of the group wrote down his own answer to the question. Because of the inherent difficulty of differentiating small differences in estimated "odds," these answers were generally stated in multiples of 0·05, i.e. 0·05, 0·10, 0·15, etc.
(c) The individual estimates and the reasons for them were discussed by the group. As a result of these discussions, differences in responses were resolved and a "group answer" was agreed upon. In almost all cases there was close agreement among salesmen in the group. In cases where differences could not be resolved, the modal (most frequent) answer was usually adopted as the group estimate.

Following the meeting with the five "outside" salesmen, a similar all-day session was held with the company's two "inside" sales engineers. The same procedure was followed and a separate series of probability estimates was obtained. Finally, a meeting was held with both the "outside" and the "inside" sales groups to resolve the two sets of estimates into a single set. Each participant was given a list of the figures derived from the two group sessions and a single figure was agreed upon for each of the probability estimates required in the analysis.

The decision model was now programmed for simulation of the various alternatives on an electronic computer. The calculations involved were not individually complex, but the large number of "branches" on the "decision tree" precluded manual computation of the results.

The procedure followed in the computer simulation was essentially as follows:

(*a*) For each price alternative, the sequence of possible subsequent events, together with the appropriate probability estimates, was laid out.

(*b*) Each price alternative was traced through to reach its possible results in terms of sales and profits. The total (cumulative compounded value at the end of five years) profit associated with each outcome was then computed.

(*c*) Probabilities for each final result were computed by multiplying out the probabilities of the events leading up to it.

(*d*) For each price alternative, the expected value of compounded net profits over the five-year planning period was computed.

The computations, on a 6 per cent basis, yielded the following estimates of expected cumulative net profits for the five-year planning period:

Price	Total net profit valued at end of period
$	$
1·00	6,625,000
0·93	7,575,000
0·85	8,475,000
0·80	8,725,000

Figure 9.5 shows these differences in compounded net profit for each price reduction, in comparison with the *status quo* price of $1·00, on a year-by-year basis. When results for the two alternative interest rates (6 per cent and 10 per cent) and for the three industry sales forecasts were examined, it was found that differences in these factors did not affect the rank order of the four price strategies. Consequently, all results were given on the basis of a 6 per cent interest rate using the "most probable" sales forecast.

Clearly, on this evidence, a price reduction on Kromel was desirable. Some uncertainty remained, however, about the validity of certain key assumptions used in the model. Most important, some executives were not convinced that an immediate price reduction would, in fact, be effective in discouraging the growth of the total industry production capacity. Accordingly, a separate series of computations was carried out assuming that price reductions would

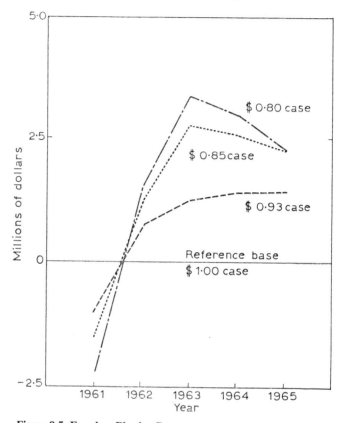

Figure 9.5 Everclear Plastics Company: compounded year-by-year net profits on Kromel

(Compound rate equals 6% annually)

not discourage additions to capacity. The estimated total net profits for Everclear, based on this revised assumption, were as follows:

Price	Total net profit valued at end of period
$	$
1·00	6,625,000
0·93	6,725,000
0·85	6,850,000
0·80	6,300,000

At this point it became clear that the key factor underlying the differences in total net profit previously estimated was Everclear's share of total Kromel industry sales. If it were assumed that a price reduction *would* discourage additions to capacity, then Everclear would probably achieve a higher share of the expanding market by reducing prices. On the other hand, if capacity were increased despite the price reduction by Everclear, the increased volume of sales—resulting from the penetration of the OEM automobile upholstery market—would just about balance the lower revenue per unit, and the expected pay-offs on alternative price strategies would be much more nearly equal. What would you, the reader of this book, have done if you had been in Everclear's position?

9.6 The Checking of Invoices and Bills

All organizations have some routine for checking and paying the bills which they incur. This may seem a trivial affair, but throughout the world there must be millions of people engaged upon the meticulous examination of documents and accounts. In many cases the scrutiny is costing more than the mistakes found thereby are worth. The typical sequence of events is:

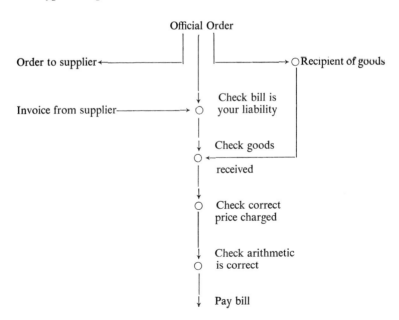

Four checks are therefore involved:

(*a*) Ensuring bill is your liability,
(*b*) Ensuring goods were received and correct,
(*c*) Ensuring correct price was charged,
(*d*) Ensuring arithmetic on invoice was correct.

A study made of these checks in the supplies department of a large local authority has been described by R. A. Ward (Director of the Local Government Operational Research Unit).

After discussion it was decided that check (*a*) had to be retained at 100 per cent, and attention was accordingly transferred to the other three checks. Consider what would happen if, instead of asking the recipient of goods to confirm all deliveries, he were required simply to report when defective deliveries had occurred, so that payment could be stopped when the invoice was received. If this principle were adopted, the bill would be passed for payment without confirmation of delivery. If the delivery failed completely, however, the recipient would also remain silent, believing that the goods were still due to arrive. Lost goods might then be paid for by the purchasing section in the mistaken belief that they had been received in good condition and on time.

By examining the extent to which goods had been lost in the past, it was possible to derive Figure 9.6. In this figure it was assumed that selective checking would be on the most expensive invoices first. For example, against 12 per cent the result shown implies that all invoices above £50 in value were checked. When the balance was struck, by adding together the losses and clerical costs shown from the figure, the optimum point of balance did, in fact, come out at 12 per cent. The incidence of overcharging which occurred on invoices was next examined. The frequency of such mistakes was again small and, by a coincidence, the optimum cost balance once more corresponded to a checking rate of the 12 per cent most valuable invoices.

Finally, the incidence of arithmetical errors was examined. Here an interesting phenomenon, shown in Figure 9.7, emerged. At first sight, it might be expected that such errors would occur completely by chance and tend to cancel one another out. In turn, this would suggest that arithmetical errors are not worth looking for, since in the long run the gains would cancel the losses. A thorough examination of the situation, however, showed that the elimination of checking led to quite serious losses. Even more surprising is the fact that a 25 per cent check produces a slight profit which is not obtained on a 100 per cent check. This must be due to the fact that the direction of the errors tends to be correlated with the size of the invoice, with the consequence that undercharging is more likely to occur on low-value invoices than on high-value invoices. In turn, this points out a feature of operational research worth stressing, namely that a thorough and quantitative examination of a familiar idea can sometimes produce a remarkable new insight. The decision taken here was to continue with the 12 per cent sample check.

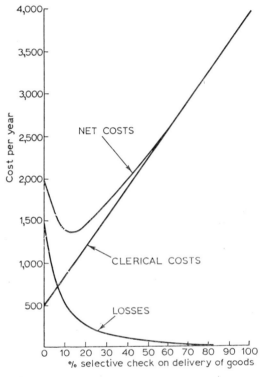

Figure 9.6 The effect of selective checking for receipt of goods on losses and clerical costs

The results of this study have now been implemented by the council concerned, and similar schemes are being introduced by other authorities. The estimated savings as a result of two years' successful operation in this one council is over £10,000, and if one looks at Local Authorities as a whole with their annual expenditure exceeding £500 m., the total saving is likely to come into the £m. category.

Clearly, organizations who adopt these techniques must not lose control. To safeguard against this, selective and purposive checking of this kind must always be coupled with a small random check. In this case, one in twenty of all low-value invoices receive meticulous attention and all errors found in this random sample are carefully

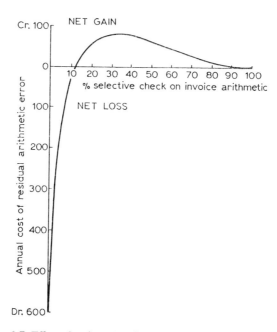

Figure 9.7 Effect of various checking levels on residual arithmetic error

recorded. By means of this controlling check, an estimate is kept on the level of errors which are occurring and special action can be initiated to follow up suspect cases. To conclude: the whole process consists of two parts—a selective check on the 12 per cent most valuable invoices and a random check on 5 per cent of the remainder.

REFERENCES

(1) Programming the allocation of funds subject to restrictions on reported results, by D. J. Chambers, *Operational Research Quarterly*, Vol. 18, No. 4, December, 1967, pp. 407–432.

(2) Building up a sequence of optimum media schedules, by D. M. Ellis, *Operational Research Quarterly*, Vol. 17, No. 4, December 1966, pp. 413–424.

(3) A computer assessment of media schedules, by E. M. L. Beale, P. A. B. Hughes and S. R. Broadbent, *Operational Research Quarterly*, Vol. 17, No. 4, December 1966, pp. 381–412.

(4) *An Application of Bayesian Decision Theory to a Problem in Long-range*

Pricing Strategy by P. E. Green, 121st Annual Meeting of American Statistical Association, December 1961.
(5) *Research for Marketing Decisions* by P. E. Green and D. S. Tull (Wiley 1966).
(6) *Developing Operational Research in Local Government* by R. A. Ward, O.E.C.D. Symposium on Contribution of Operational Research to Urban and Regional Planning, December 1966.

10 Implementation and the Future

I. Methods of Analysis

10.1 Comprehensive Models

Broadly speaking, all models used in describing operational research problems fall into one of three different categories: *iconic models, analogue models*, and *symbolic models*.

Iconic models are representations of states, objects, or events. As they represent the relevant properties of the real thing, with only some form of scale transformation of these properties, iconic models look like what they represent. For example, road maps and aerial photographs represent distances between, and relative positions of, places and the routes between them. Flow charts which show the processing of material or information may also be iconic, as may be floor plans or other types of diagram. In many cases where it is desired to show a third dimension on a map, the procedure is not to use the third dimension as such, but to resort to colours or contour lines which by their distance apart convey information about rates of change. In such cases one property is being used to represent another and hence the necessity for some kind of legend. In these cases the model takes on an analogue form.

Probably the most familiar form of analogue model is that of the slide rule, in which quantities are represented by distances which are proportionate to their logarithms. But the principle can be taken considerably further, with electronic circuits being used to solve various equations, for example. Thus the simple exponential smoothing equation for forecasting described in Chapter 7 can be solved by having an electronic circuit with the appropriate responses and delays built into it so that, by feeding in the basic data concerning the smoothing constant, the current forecast, and the current demand, the new forecast can be obtained.

Thirdly, there are symbolic models, in which the properties of the items represented are expressed symbolically. Thus a relationship which is shown in a graph in iconic form can also be shown in an equation as a symbolic model. Models in which the symbols employed represent quantities are usually called mathematical models.

Iconic models are the most specific and concrete of the three types, but are usually the most difficult to manipulate when determining the effect of changes in the basic situation. For example, examining a graph in which distance and time are plotted is unlikely to produce precise numerical answers to problems unless the graph has been clearly and appropriately labelled. In the analogue model, properties that are easier to manipulate are substituted for the real properties. As a consequence, such models are more abstract and general. Symbolic models are the most abstract and general and the easiest to manipulate. The amount of effort required to construct a model is inversely related, broadly, to the ease of manipulating it once it has been constructed. Generally, iconic and analogue models are a preliminary step towards the development of an appropriate symbolic model.

Any model constructed to represent a problem situation is only an approximation and is generally simpler than the situation it seeks to represent. Of course, the latter is usually so complex that an exact representation, even if possible, would lead to hopeless mathematical complexity. Hence the problem which concerns the model-builder is to obtain the best, or at least a reasonable, balance between accurate representations and mathematical manageability. Practical considerations such as time, money, personnel, or computing facilities would almost always require some compromise of accuracy. This manageability is of two types, one involving the researcher and the other the decision-maker. On the one hand, construction of a model that the researcher cannot solve because of its mathematical complexity is of little value. On the other hand, the derivation of a solution which is too complex mathematically for the decision-maker to use is also of little value. The simplifying assumptions on which the model is based should be made explicit, so that the researcher can determine in what direction the problem is falsified and by how much. Such a determination is essential in justifying the approximation of the model.

Approximations can be used in two different ways in the construction of models. First, they can be used to "sneak up" on a problem by building successively more complex approximations. To quote G. D. Camp: "I prefer to start with two or a small number of the crudest and simplest models which appear to offer any hope of representing the major features of the operation under study, choosing them so as to surround the real operation as well as possible. These models can usually be operated by simple desk calculations, the results being used to judge the desirability for further refinements and the directions which these should take if deemed desirable." The other approach is to proceed from a model that is too complex to handle to successively simpler approximations, until one is obtained that is both manageable and accurate enough. Whether one should approximate up or down is largely a matter for personal preference and the complexity of the problem at hand. Ideally the result should be the same whichever approach is adopted, although the amount of effort involved may be considerably different.

10.2   The Variables Included

One important factor to bear in mind in the design of any model is that increasing the number of variables affects the work involved by a more than proportionate amount. To this end, variables are often aggregated, and it is important to be able to estimate the errors caused by such aggregation. For example, packaging, storage, and distribution problems often involve hundreds of different products, each in several different packings, and hence thousands of variables may be required for a precise representation. A brief examination of the packages concerned will often show, however, that they can be grouped by classes, either according to the facilities used to package them, or to their weight, or to their value, etc. The effect of such aggregation can then be estimated. The groupings are chosen in such a way as to put together items with an approximate similarity of properties, so that the variability of these properties inside the group is relatively small compared with the whole set of items, and the variation then plays much the same role as do fluctuations in arrival rate at a queue. For example, if one million pint cans of different lubricating oils must be canned per month, it makes little difference what kinds of oils go into the cans provided batch sizes are reasonably large. Owing to differences in viscosity, canning rates may be different, but good bounds will be obtained by grouping the kinds of oil and using the appropriate average and variability measures to get the necessary limits.

It is common practice to ignore many of the constraints in the initial solution of a model and to see whether the solution to this partly constrained problem happens in fact to satisfy most or all of the constraints. In general, the omission of constraints yields an optimistic solution, whilst the addition of constraints yields a pessimistic solution. Consequently, by manipulation of the constraints, upper and lower bounds on the problem solution can be obtained. Problem situations are frequently so complicated that one model of the entire situation cannot feasibly be constructed. In such cases the problem may be broken into parts so that each part can be modelled separately. The interactions between the outputs of the models are specified and taken into account. For example, consider a problem involving the determination of the number of maintenance shops which an army should have in order to service construction equipment. Here two models are required, with the output from the first model forming the input to the second. The first model is constructed so as to determine, for a specified number of shops, the optimum number of men to be assigned to each shop, noting that the amount of equipment waiting for repairs decreases as the work force increases. The model minimizes the sum of the shop cost together with the queue or waiting-line costs. This model is used repetitively for a range of assumed numbers of shops. For each assumption the minimal total cost is computed and these results then become the input to a second model used for determining the optimal total number of shops.

10.3 Methods of Solution

Solutions may be derived from the formulated models along three major lines. These are: (*a*) analytic, (*b*) numerical, and (*c*) simulation. Illustrations of each of these methods have been given earlier in this book, but some general comments follow.

(*a*) *Analytic methods*
If the model consists of an equation with merely one controllable variable, then the optimizing value, assuming that one exists, can be determined by mathematical methods. If there are two or more controllable variables, the procedure can still be used and, even if the controllable variables have some constraints or restrictions put on them by one or more equations or inequalities, there are mathematical methods available to handle the situation. In some cases an optimum value for a function, rather than an individual variable, is required. In theory there are mathematical methods available for such situations, but in practice only a few problems can be solved along these lines. Normally it is necessary to resort to numerical techniques in such cases, particularly the techniques of mathematical programming.

(*b*) *Numerical methods*
The familiar trial-and-error procedure is an example of a numerical procedure. With the help of graphical plots it is often possible to determine rapidly the neighbourhood of the optimum of some system and concentrate further trials in that region. Since trial-and-error can be very time-consuming, efforts have been made to modify these procedures so that the trials converge to a solution. Such procedures involve the repetition of a well-defined sequence of steps

until a solution is obtained, and they are often referred to as iterative procedures. Thus the standard methods of linear programming are designed on an iterative basis to get quickly to the solution, starting from some feasible solution found by other means. An alternative form of algebra (called Boolean algebra) has been used to reduce logically the number of possible solutions when the number of possibilities is absolutely immense, since even with an electronic computer the complete set would take a long time to evaluate.

(c) *Simulation*

An essential characteristic of simulation is contained in the observation that "whilst a model represents a phenomenon, simulation attempts to imitate it." This dynamic aspect of simulation is also revealed by the comment that "whereas models are photographs simulations are motion pictures." Thus models and simulations should be contrasted, in that simulation is a way of using a model so that experimentation can be made on the model rather than on the phenomenon itself. In theory, everything that can be accomplished by simulation can be accomplished by experimenting directly on the phenomenon involved in the problem. In practice, however, it is often impossible, or at any rate impracticable, to experiment on the phenomenon itself. Even when analysts have the confidence and ability to arrive at a theoretical prediction of the behaviour of some large system, it may not be possible to perform validating experiments. You cannot, for example, test conclusions about the possible strategies for global wars by trying them out even once. When any difficulties of this type occur, as they must do in tackling previously untouched and unmanageable problems, some form of simulation is the obvious tool to be tried. Simulation involves the use of numbers and hence is an extended form of a type of numerical analysis. In a numerical analysis, the numerical values of the controlled and uncontrolled variables are inserted in the model and the outcome is calculated by normal arithmetical operations. By trying a number of possible combinations of numerical values for the variables, the best combination can be identified and selected. In simulation a number of solutions are again tried, but the difference from normal numerical procedures lies in the way in which the solution is evaluated. The evaluation or testing of a proposed solution to a decision model consists of running the system on paper, or on a computer, for a set of values of the controlled variables that generate enough instances of outcomes so that their distribution can be determined. From these observations, the required parameters can be estimated.

For example, in a queueing problem, it has already been mentioned that it may not be possible to determine analytically how many serving facilities there ought to be in order to minimize the total cost of operation. For any specified number of facilities, however, the operation can be run on paper by imitating the arrival of customers, their queueing, their selection of service, their servicing, and their departure. By observing these operations, the distribution of possible outcomes can be estimated, together with the costs of operation and the value of the measure of performance based on it. The principle of simulation does not require a computer, although in many instances the degree of simulation required is such that the problem would become relatively unmanageable unless a computer were available. It should, however, be noted that where a computer is used, several hand runs of the simulation are usually required to check the computer program, and these runs can also be employed to arrive at some crude estimate of the number of simulations that are required to obtain the results, with due consideration of economy as well as of accuracy. It should be pointed out that the cost of using a computer involves not only the running time but also the initial programming and the inevitable debugging. The simulation must therefore be of a reasonably complex and lengthy situation before the use of a computer involves less human effort than does hand computation.

II. Implementation

10.4 The Importance of Implementation

A great deal of emphasis is rightly placed in all operational research courses and books on the necessity for care in problem recognition and problem definition. It is, however, becoming increasingly clear that there is an even more important facet of operational research work, namely the manner by which the implementation of the results is approached. The basic aim of operational research is to improve on some situation. Hence unless a solution is implemented, little is achieved. There is a fantastic mobility amongst operational research workers. With this mobility has grown an impression that one of the causes of the movement is the difficulty operational research workers have found in getting solutions implemented, with the consequent feeling that the grass is greener in the next field. The solutions they provide may be improvements, but the organization prefers its present ways as being more comfortable for all concerned.

Skills and techniques help the manager by supplying him with a more sophisticated means of separating facts from the subjective elements; computers, sampling techniques, and linear programming can all give more or less reliable data to supplant the hunches or informed guesses of the old-style business man. However, his present day counterpart still has to evaluate the significance and the reliability of such data and especially the assumptions on which the data were built up. The danger about all results obtained from computers and models of all kinds is that they look impressively neat and infallible; yet they are often based at key points on purely subjective judgments which afterwards tend to be overlooked. Mathematical models will only give results consistent with the assumption fed in. This is not to deny their value, as they sharpen the manager's awareness of the issues involved in a problem. There will still remain certain subjective factors and it is perhaps in this area that the clash between the operational researcher and the manager is most likely to occur.

The communication and persuasion problems which exist between the organization as a whole and the operational research worker within it are the visible signs of the difficulty, but any solution must go far beyond the trite formulae "let the manager learn science" or "let the scientist learn how to sell." Behind these visible signs lie the twin horns of the politics of the organization and the unconscious thought processes of those within it. To the consciously observing mind of the scientist, a great deal of managerial activity is political, and the reasons given for any action seem rarely to be the real reasons; the latter are almost always unconscious. On the other hand, once a decision has been made, the manager seeks to find perfectly conscious and justifiable reasons why this decision is the best one. These reasons will be contained in statements made to the employees, to the press, to directors, etc.

The scientist may sometimes abhor what he thinks of as either dishonesty, or at least self-deception, in the managerial decision-making process. But he should have the honesty to realize that his own way of arranging his affairs is basically little different. Indeed, science can be inconsistently proud of the mysteries of its own unconscious life. Science knows very little about its own basic decision-making processes; how new ideas are created, how trends in research effort are established, how a decision to open a new line of attack on a problem is agreed, how the resistance set up to radical ideas is overcome. But once a project is under way, science can call into play all its rational background: objective evidence, mathematical models, experimental design, rigorous analysis, etc.

Much of the discussion about the inter-relationship of science and management is concerned with the comparison of the rational, conscious, and apolitical sides of each. Operational research attempts to modify the reasoning and justification processes of management by putting them in the setting of finer and more elaborate models than the manager can usually create by himself. Once the basic political and unconscious decision has been made, management can only be grateful to the scientist who subsequently adds such magnificent strength to the justification process. Thus, if it has been decided on political grounds to build a motorway through part of a city, the authorities are grateful to anyone who sets out to minimize delays on the entrances and exists; they help to provide an excellent justification for the design.

Neither managers nor scientists really want to understand their own unconscious thought processes. Managers refer to these processes as being intuitive or from experience, whilst scientists refer to them as being creative. Managers claim that no one is ever going to be able to put their decision-making effectively on to computers; scientists claim that the creative process of genius is an eternal mystery (some would go as far as to say that it possesses a random element). Hence mutual understanding calls for an intellectual attack upon the mysteries of both management and science. On the side of management it calls for an understanding of the politics of decision-making, and on the side of science it calls for an understanding of the creative process. This call is threatening to both. Yet the scientist must surely feel uncomfortable if he is forced to regard himself as someone who merely finds justifications for managers' decisions. At the same time the manager himself may well feel uncomfortable if he dwells on the thought that a large part of his research support goes into activities that cannot be closely analysed, and therefore cannot be controlled.

Movement towards this "mutual understanding" relationship and away from the "separate function" relationship can take place only slowly and has not yet occurred to any significant extent in the vast bulk of organizations. To achieve it requires a sequence of events:

(a) Progress towards the communication and persuasion types of relationship,
(b) Re-appraisal of the power differential between the researcher and the manager,
(c) An increase in the consensus of opinion as to the value of mutual co-operation,
(d) A growth in mutual respect.

Thus the problems of implementation are of great importance to the esteem of all concerned and, furthermore, should be thought about at the commencement of any study and not left until the end. Impressive solutions to operational research problems are sometimes found, and then left in a non-implemented state, simply because the company concerned does not work in the manner assumed by the solution, and to change it to the manner required would mean an alteration in company policy or management practices which it is not willing to countenance. The operational research team has, in such cases, been unable to establish full rapport with company thinking at a sufficiently early stage. This may be, and sometimes is, because the company "holds its cards close to its chest" and does not take the operational research team fully into its confidence. It may, alternatively, be due to the team's racing through its understanding of the problem too quickly, and thus failing to appreciate the way management thinks and acts in the particular organization concerned. Finally, it is necessary to establish some means of monitoring the performance of any new systems or working methods established. Only by such means can valuable lessons be learnt for application to future work.

III. The Future Role of Operational Research

10.5   The Role of Operational Research

There is little doubt that operational research has arrived in this country and is very much part of the management services available to the executive. Operational research has made worthwhile contributions to problems such as allocation and distribution, to marketing procedures, to the analysis of risk in capital investment, to the allocation of funds for media planning, to the optimization of inventory holdings, to the scheduling of toll booths on tunnels and motorways, and to the minimization of the number of drill holes required when exploring for nickel or other minerals. Demand for operational research practitioners far exceeds the supply, with the result that there is need for management to practise economy to ensure the most effective use of the skills available and to ensure the choice of the correct practitioner.

Table 10.1 shows the growth in the number of members of the United Kingdom Operational Research Society over the last ten years. Full membership denotes that the Society accepts the member as having acquired a reasonable level of competence and experience in the subject; associate members need only demonstrate an interest in the subject. The growth rate is extremely high and even that of full members is approximately 10 per cent per annum. The numbers themselves must, however, be set off against the number of companies there are in the country. If *all* the full members were concentrated, rather unexpectedly, in the three hundred top companies listed by

TABLE 10.1

Membership of Operational Research Society

Year	Full members	Associate members	Total
1956	203	84	287
1958	255	225	480
1960	284	367	651
1962	320	598	918
1964	394	834	1,259*
1966	503	1,497	2,057*
1967	536	1,766	2,367*

* Includes collective members.

The Times, there would be only one such member per £40 million of capital employed. If those employed in teaching and in government or by nationalized industries are deducted, a truer figure is probably nearer one full member per £50 million of capital. Thus the United Steel Company would be "entitled" to three members, Cunard Steam-Ship Company two, Fisons one, and some 125 companies of the 300 wouldn't even rate half a member. They include companies such as Rugby Portland Cement and W. H. Smith! Although this analysis points out the relative dearth of experienced men, it would be unfortunate and completely erroneous if it gave the impression that operational research cannot help the medium or smaller sized firm. It can do so, and is doing so in numerous instances.

The aim of any business must primarily be to make profits, whilst that of its management is to make decisions and control the enterprise to achieve that aim, largely by working through people. The success of management in years past has been primarily related to its ability to apply skilled judgment to all facets of a problem simultaneously. This is no longer as practicable as formerly, in that many problems are now so complex that it is impossible for one mind to comprehend the full range of possibilities, thus necessitating some formal and systematic approach to rational decision-making.

In recent years management has been inundated with a plethora of experts each claiming to be able to resolve the more intractable of the business's problems—management accounting, work study, organization and methods, and so on. Hence any claim to provide a global service to management must be treated with caution and carefully tested. Many disciplines have contributed to the management services' mosaic: mathematics, statistics, probability, economics amongst them, and it would seem only natural and desirable that all these subjects should expand their horizons and integrate more fully with each other. Operational research has attempted over the last fifteen years to supply the necessary integrative force but, in so doing, it has come to a cross-roads in its existence and development. It can either seek to become a global discipline of quantitative decision analysis embracing the subjects outlined in earlier sections, or it can aim to become a specific management service embracing organization problems and behavioural problems as well as work study, mathematics, statistics, etc. If it chooses the former it will find itself overlapping a variety of well-established disciplines, while if it chooses the latter it will cease to be moving towards a discipline, but towards a vocational subject. In the same way, the vocation of surveying is related to the disciplines of mathematics, physics, chemistry, etc.

At the moment operational research shows signs of trying to ride both horses simultaneously, but this is fraught with dangers and it must decide upon its direction. The interests and activities shown currently by the United Kingdom Operational Research Society, and the natural desires of management, suggest that it would achieve the most by moving towards the vocational end of the scale. One could go as far as saying that if it became a discipline, and automatically more academic, there would be a danger of yet another management science springing up to fill the gap. If this is indeed so, one incidental consequence will be that a great deal of careful thought will be required to rationalize the present plethora of courses in operational research in this country, many of which provide a rag-bag of assorted techniques. If, however, operational research is to become a discipline, it seems that it can do so only by capturing the generalized quantitative decision area, much of which is currently split between the mathematician, the statistician, the economist, and the financial analyst.

10.6   Organization

Writing in 1959, Patrick Rivett, now Professor of Operational Research at the University of Sussex, pointed out that the vast majority of operational research workers were employed by industrial concerns. This formed one of the then major differences between operational research in the United States as opposed to the United Kingdom, in that the effort in the United States also extended to both the universities and management consultants. Conditions have changed considerably in this country during the intervening years, and the pattern here is now becoming much more American;

indeed, relatively few of the big names in operational research in this country are currently employed by industrial organizations. The reasons for this change are open to speculation, but one possibility which is strongly canvassed is that the range and variety of intellectual challenges that a university or consulting firm can offer is probably greater than in most industrial concerns, and the type of man who is best attracted into operational research needs this continual challenge.

Nevertheless, the vast bulk of large companies do have operational research groups of varying sizes, and their organization brings problems. The three main problems involved are the group's location within the organization, the personnel to be employed, and the method of working. It is an essential part of the success of an operational research group that its members should have access to all parts of the organization and be considered as an adjunct to the management team. Provided that this criterion is satisfied, and the operational research group is able to report direct to all people concerned with the problem being tackled, then the actual location of the group within the parent organization is of lesser importance. Clearly the decision as to its location must depend upon company practice, and it is dangerous and equivocal to give the group a location that is denied to other management service functions. Experience has shown that the commonly canvassed possibility of locating the group within the ordinary scientific research department of a company can be a great handicap. Although the group is primarily a scientific activity, the field of problems studied and the time scale within which the work has to be completed are generally so different from the normal run of research work that the two sides have very diverse objectives. The overriding consideration, though, in deciding the location is to enable it to have close relations with other management specialities, without destroying its distinctive quality by merging it with such subjects as Work Study or Organization and Methods. It is, however, essential that the group has the ear of the correct level of operating management, and one effective way in which this can be done is to have the group reporting to an advisory board made up of managers from each of the principal departments of the company. This should be a permanent board that continues from project to project, meeting with the group for periodical reviews of progress every six weeks or so. Views on alternative locations are likely to continue to differ in the future, and much must depend upon the individual personalities involved, together with the capabilities of the managers who have to control the various departmental activities.

An alternative way to look at this dilemma is to accept that a

pressing need today is for management to be provided with a pro-
fessionally qualified management services "brain-centre." The way
in which computers have developed within many large organizations
demonstrates this need very clearly. In some organizations, computers and data processing have grown up very much on a decentralized, or divisional, basis with the curious result that in many
instances common definitions are not being used, computers do
not provide back-up facilities for each other, there is no ability to

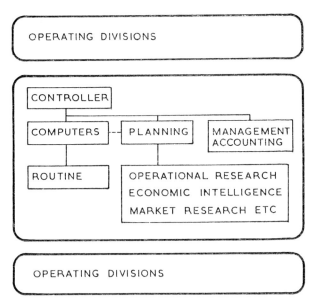

Figure 10.1 The business "brain-centre" concept

sort and collate material from out-stations automatically, and so
forth. The net result is recognized after a time as being wasteful
and uneconomic. This then leads to the need for a centrally co-
ordinated computer function with the computer (or computers)
being used not only for the various routine operations, but also for
the assistance that they can provide in a planning role. The latter
is closely allied to the operational research function, just as the
management accounting function is linked to it. Given a business
which has a number of separate operating (or functional) divisions,
a possible form of organization which seeks to draw together the
interested activities into a further division, headed by a controller,
is shown in Figure 10.1.

10.7 The Selection of Personnel

If this kind of organization is to become viable, the operational research worker needs to regard himself as taking part in a vocational experience which draws in the ideas, tools, and methodologies of a large number of disciplines, ranging from some of the relatively imprecise (at present) areas of psychology to the more precise areas of mathematics. But, in carrying out such a function, the individual must show himself willing to sacrifice the notion of "optimality or nothing" which has sometimes plagued operational research. This in turn requires him to refrain from aiming to make one specific recommendation on every problem and to assume the (deceptively) more modest role of producing relevant information intended to facilitate the manager's own decision-making. The term "information" is used here in a wide sense to include such concepts as an "outcome matrix," i.e. a display of the outcomes of alternative policies where outcomes may be expressed in terms of multiple criteria. The emphasis would then be on conditional rather than factual information; there would not necessarily be a single criterion, and consequently no unique concept, of optimality. The investigation would provide the manager with a number of "if—then" statements and manager acceptance might well be considerably enhanced. By such means it would be possible for operational research to provide a valuable service in marrying together the power which can be brought to a problem from various basic disciplines, thus overcoming some of the difficulties of communication discussed earlier in this chapter.

Traditionally, disciplines have kept themselves fairly separate and developed along individual lines. Many barriers have been broken in recent years and it is noteworthy, as evidence of this trend, how many people have now acquired membership of more than one professional society. Assuming operational research becomes basically a vocational subject embracing all sides of a management service activity, it is immediately apparent that not every worker within such an activity can expect to know all parts of the subject area equally well. Conversely, those workers coming from one individual discipline, whilst being capable of operating as specialists in their own discipline, must be aware of, and sympathetic to, other parts of the management service spectrum. This suggests that individuals coming through separate disciplines to professional status need to be provided with some formal training and experience in those concomitant areas to be fully effective in management services.

It has been suggested that, in setting up an operational research group, the first six personnel appointed should have the following distinctive backgrounds: a physical scientist, an engineer, a statistician or mathematician, a behavioural scientist, a specialist in scientific methodology, and a company-oriented man. As the group grows beyond this size, the weightings given to different parts of this disciplinary breakdown would very likely change according to the type of work carried out. In an article in 1965, Stafford Beer, then the head of a consulting firm markedly biased towards operational research, gave the following breakdown of the primary qualification of the 50 professional staff in his organization:

Physical and engineering sciences   34%
Biological and human sciences   24%
Mathematics, statistics, and logic   26%
Philosophy, politics, and economics 16%

It is a generally accepted principle that the group ought to be as diverse in its background as possible, in that the many different types of activity which become integrated in the overall approach that is characteristic of the operational research field require many specialists of varying basic disciplines.

Management service specialists suffer, too, from having great power in an analytical sense, but without real long-term responsibility in the way the manager understands the term. This emphasizes the need for firms to have a rotational plan, similar to the career planning in the Armed Services, whereby some men go out from the "brain-centre" to gain line experience, not just at the top but lower down, and then possibly return at some later stage. It is frequently said that "scientists" are virtually burnt out at 30. This is not basically true in operational research, which seeks to marry the objectivity of science with the subjectivity of the manager's experience. Two-way movement of personnel is a desirable feature of the effective utilization of operational research practitioners. The shortage of such personnel is probably one reason why such rotational plans are rare. But, if carried out systematically, such plans can enhance the effectiveness of the brain-centre as well as providing a further training ground for top management material.

Appendix A
The Simplex Method for Linear Programming

A.1 Introduction

The standard algebraic technique used for solving linear programming problems is known as the Simplex method. Essentially the method consists of defining the problem in a standard form, and then finding by inspection a feasible solution (i.e. a solution that satisfies all the conditions and constraints, but does not necessarily produce maximum profit, assuming profit to be the quantity that is to be optimized). This first feasible solution is then amended by a series of steps, each step being chosen so as to improve the profit until a situation is reached where no further improvement can be achieved. The procedure is, therefore, an iterative one which satisfies the conditions:

(a) There is a mathematical rule which determines after each step exactly what the next step is to be, on the basis of the step just completed (a consequence of this feature is that it makes electronic computation possible);
and

(b) The method is constructed in such a way that it guarantees that each trial yields values which are closer to the final answer than the preceding ones.

The details of the method are best illustrated through an example.

A.2 The Simplex Procedure

To keep the problem simple and also to be able to demonstrate the solution graphically, as well as algebraically, the problem used will again be a two-product one, but on this occasion the method is capable of generalization to three or more types. The following illustration, of a product mix problem, relates to the manufacture of two products, 1 and 2, which use the same two sequential processes,

TABLE A.1

Basic Data

Process	Processing time per unit (hours)		Maximum available processing time (hours)
	1 Product 2		
A	4	2	24
B	3	6	36
Profit per unit (£)	3	2	—

A and B. The processing times are given in Table A.1., together with the available time and profits.

Put formally, it is desired to maximize the profit function:

$$P = 3x_1 + 2x_2 \tag{i}$$

where x_1 and x_2 are the number of units made of products 1 and 2 respectively, subject to the constraints:

Process A $4x_1 + 2x_2 \leqslant 24$ (ii)

Process B $3x_1 + 6x_2 \leqslant 36$ (iii)

where the symbol $\leqslant$ is the mathematical shorthand for "less than or equal to."

The solution proceeds by a series of steps.

Step 1

Write the capacity restrictions in the form of equations of equality by adding a "slack variable" to each equation. Then:

(ii) becomes $4x_1 + 2x_2 + x_3 = 24$ (iv)

(iii) becomes $3x_1 + 6x_2 + x_4 = 36$ (v)

x_3 represents the quantity of a fictitious product with unit processing time which utilizes the available unused capacity (if any) in process A; x_4 performs a similar role for process B.

Step 2

Construct an array, referred to as a "matrix," of the coefficients of these equations of restrictions, labelling the columns with the appropriate variables. The rows are labelled with the appropriate slack variables and maximum capacity, as shown in Table A.2.

TABLE A.2

Matrix for Step 2

Variable	Capacity	3	2	0	0
		x_1	x_2	x_3	$x,$
Process A $\quad x_3$	24	4	2	1	0
Process B $\quad x_4$	36	3	6	0	1

3 2 0 0 ←—Coefficients of profit function

Initial solution

Rates of substitution

The two left-hand columns in Table A.2 give the values of the non-zero variables in the current solution. Thus initially a solution with $x_3 = 24$, $x_4 = 36$ units is chosen, which means that there is no production and no profit. (Note that the number of non-zero variables does not exceed the number of constraints and that these constraints, defined by equations (iv) and (v), are satisfied. Such a solution is called a "basic feasible solution.")

The matrix array can then be interpreted in the following manner. If a unit of product 1 is made, this will displace 4 units of product 3 and 3 units of product 4. Since the unit profits associated with the products 1, 3 and 4 are 3, 0 and 0 respectively, then the opportunity profit associated with making one unit of product 1 is

$$(3 \times 1) - (4 \times 0) - (3 \times 0) = 3$$

Similarly, the opportunity profits for the other column variables can be calculated and are 2, 0 and 0 for the products 2, 3 and 4 respectively. The solution which must be tested for optimality is shown in the left-hand side.

As stated above, with this initial solution, there is no production and no profit.

Step 3

Calculate the opportunity profits for each column variable and identify the column with the greatest positive opportunity profit. This is known as the pivotal column. Divide the coefficients in the capacity column by the respective coefficients in the pivotal column. Identify the row with the smallest positive value so calculated. This is known as the pivotal row, and the coefficient at the intersection of this row and column is known as the pivot. Table A.3 illustrates the procedure.

This process is the mathematical equivalent of saying that Product 1 offers the greatest opportunity to increase profits, but that no more than $6(= 24/4)$ units can be made without exceeding the capacity available from process A.

TABLE A.3
Matrix for Step 3

Variable	Capacity	3 x_1	2 x_2	0 x_3	0 x_4	Profit per unit
x_3	24	(4)	2	1	0	$24/4 = 6$ (Pivot row)
x_4	36	3	6	0	1	$36/3 = 12$
Opportunity profit		3	2	0	0	

(Pivot
column)

Step 4
Next construct a new matrix array of coefficients from the existing one by following these rules:

(*a*) The pivot row is reconstructed by dividing all the coefficients in it (including the capacity label in that row) by the pivot coefficient.

(*b*) Calculate the new coefficients of the other row(s) of the array by subtracting from each such row the reconstructed pivot row multiplied by the coefficient lying in the row being transformed and in the pivot column. This ensures that the pivot, which now has the value 1, is the only non-zero coefficient in the pivot column.

The result of these calculations is shown in Table A.4 below.

TABLE A.4
Matrix for Step 4

Variable	Capacity	3 x_1	2 x_2	0 x_3	0 x_4	Profit per unit
x_1	6	1	$\frac{1}{2}$	$\frac{1}{4}$	0	$6 \times 2 = 12$
x_4	18	0	$(\frac{9}{2})$	$-\frac{3}{4}$	1	$18 \times 2/9 = 4$ (Pivot row)
Opportunity profit		0	$\frac{1}{2}$	$-\frac{3}{4}$	0	

(Pivot
column)

The opportunity profits are now recalculated. Thus under x_2, a unit of x_2 would displace $\frac{1}{2}$ a unit of x_1 and $\frac{9}{2}$ of a unit of x_4. Hence the profit would be $2 - \frac{1}{2} \times 3 - \frac{9}{2} \times 0$, or $\frac{1}{2}$. For x_1 the opportunity profit would be $3 - 3$, or 0, as x_1 is merely replaced by

x_1. Similarly for the other columns. The highest column opportunity profit is x_2, hence that column is the pivot. The corresponding row values will be $6/\frac{1}{2}$, or 12, and $18/\frac{9}{2}$, or 4. Hence the latter is the new pivotal row, and the value $\frac{9}{2}$ is the new pivot.

Step 5

The procedures described under steps 3 and 4 are now repeated until a matrix array is obtained which has no positive opportunity profits. At this stage there is no point in making further substitution and the optimum has been reached. In the present example, the new matrix array becomes as shown in Table A.5 and when the

TABLE A.5

Matrix for Step 5

Variable	Capacity	3 x_1	2 x_2	0 x_3	0 x_4	Profit per unit
x_1	4	1	0	$\frac{1}{3}$	$-\frac{1}{9}$	
x_2	4	0	1	$-\frac{1}{6}$	$\frac{2}{9}$	
Opportunity profit		0	0	$-\frac{2}{3}$	$-\frac{1}{9}$	

revised opportunity profits are calculated it will be seen that they are all zero or negative. Hence there is no point in making further substitution and the optimum has been reached. Under this optimum, $x_1 = 4$, $x_2 = 4$, and the profit will be

$$4 \times 3 + 4 \times 2 = 20$$

Note that from the final array, if there were a profit per unit of $\frac{1}{9}$ associated with x_4, then x_4 would have a zero opportunity profit and could be brought into the solution without decreasing the total profit. Thus if x_4 represented the amount of some product being manufactured, its price would have to be increased by this amount to make its production worthwhile. In fact, it represents the number of hours for which process B is unused, so losing an hour of process B would represent a loss of £$\frac{1}{9}$. Thus the marginal value of process B is £$\frac{1}{9}$, and similarly that of process A is £$\frac{2}{3}$.

A.3 A Graphical Analysis

Figure A.1 shows the same problem treated graphically as for the Transrad Company in Chapter 3. The constraints imposed on the capacity of the two processes as given in Table A.1, lead to capacity boundaries in Figure A.1 given by the line JK for process A and by

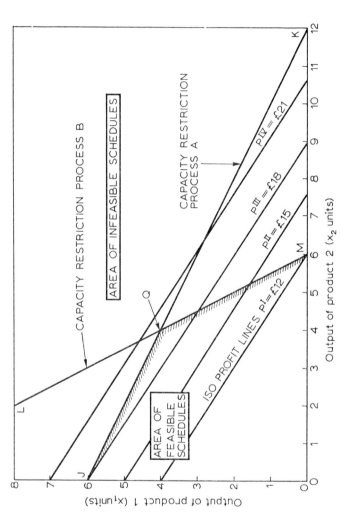

Figure A.1 Capacity relationships between two products sharing same production resources

the line LM for process B. Lines of iso-profit (i.e. the same profit for any point on the line) are shown for profits between £12 and £21 and it can be readily deduced that the point of maximum profit will be that marked Q. This corresponds to $x_1 = 4$, $x_2 = 4$ as above, giving a total profit of 20. Note that in the Simplex solution the first solution under step 2 above is the point (0, 0). The next solution under step 3 is the point J (0, 6). The third solution, step 4, is the point Q (4, 4), and step 5 shows that no further improvement can then be made.

A.4 References to Programming Techniques

The simplex technique for linear programming is fully dealt with in

Mathematical Programming by S. Vajda (Addison-Wesley 1961),

Linear Programming by G. Hadley (Addison-Wesley 1962),

Mathematical Programming in Practice by E. M. L. Beale (Pitman 1968).

There are three other forms of programming to which reference may usefully be made. The first is *quadratic programming* where the constraints amongst the variables are still linear, but the function which it is desired to maximize or minimize is quadratic amongst the variables concerned. For example, a firm produces five varieties of cakes and makes use of three types of raw material, all in limited supply. The various kinds of cakes use the raw material types in different proportions. The contribution to income depends upon the amounts produced of the five varieties and the overall profit becomes a quadratic function of the proportion of cakes produced in the five varieties. Two additional references to methods of solution for such problems are

On quadratic programming, by E. M. L. Beale, *Naval Research Logistics Quarterly*, 1959, Vol. 6, pp. 227–243.

The simplex method for quadratic programming, by P. Wolfe, *Econometrica*, 1959, Vol. 27, pp. 382–398.

The second form is *dynamic programming* which arises where the approach requires a sequence of decisions to be made. The theory is almost entirely due to Richard Bellman who states as his "principle of optimality" that an optimal policy has the property that, whatever the initial state and the initial decision, the remaining decisions must constitute an optimal policy with regard to the state resulting from the first decision. This principle can be applied to a situation where there are a number of projects, k, each having an expected value of successful outcome, and it is desired to apportion a fixed amount of effort between these projects so as to maximize the total expected gain. Another illustration of its application is in the purchase of items from a manufacturer for retail sale against a probability distribution of sales against time, with varying possibilities of being able to sell back unwanted stock. Dynamic programming can then be used to formulate an optimum buying policy. The standard text on dynamic programming is

> *Dynamic Programming* by R. E. Bellman (Oxford University Press, 1957).

The third form is *integer programming*. This is concerned with any of the types of programming already discussed but with a further restriction upon the variables concerned in the sense that the solutions must be integers. The best known problem of this nature is that of the travelling salesman. For this problem, let n towns be given together with the starting distances between all possible pairs of towns. It is required to arrange a route starting from a given town, visiting all the other towns and returning to the starting-point in such a way that the total distance travelled is as short as possible. There are $\frac{1}{2}(n-1)(n-2)\ldots(3)(2)(1)$ possible different circular tours that are essentially different and the problem is the same whatever the starting-point. This can be formulated as a linear programming problem with the additional restriction that the variables must either take a value zero or 1, according to whether or not the salesman makes the particular journey between two possible points. If no restrictions of an integer nature are placed on the problem it is quite possible to obtain absurd results by use of the ordinary linear programming techniques, i.e. fractional numbers of salesmen being sent along given routes in a particular situation. Comprehensive surveys of integer programming are given in

> *Linear Programming and Extensions* by G. B. Dantzig (Oxford University Press 1963).

> Survey of integer programming, by E. M. L. Beale, *Operational Research Quarterly* (1965), Vol. 16, pp. 219–228

Appendix B
Some Statistical Concepts

B.1 Inferential Statistics

Inferential statistics is concerned with the drawing of an inference concerning a population (or "universe" which is used as an interchangeable term with population). A universe consists of all possible objects, states, or events within defined bounds, and it may be very large or very small. If the universe is large, it may sometimes be assumed to be effectively infinite in order to ease computation without loss of accuracy. A universe may not always be large; it may be defined as only a dozen events or even as only one object. The relative usefulness of the universe as an entity will be paramount in its definition.

All males over 21 years old in the United Kingdom make up a universe. The schoolchildren in Oxford make up another. The car accidents occurring in Kent in 1967 make up yet another. All these populations are finite. They constitute populations that could, with sufficient care and patience, be counted and enumerated. In some cases they may be so large, for example the pebbles on the beach at Hastings, that they are effectively infinite and would have to be treated as such. Other populations are truly infinite. For example, the number of points on a line is infinite. The possible different lengths of life of electric light bulbs are infinite; the possible lengths of steel bars are infinite. In practice even in these cases the number of different values that can be recorded is finite, as there will always be a limit to the precision with which such quantities can be measured.

B.2 The Sample

A sample is a part or portion of a universe. It may range in size from one unit (or individual) to one less than the number of units in the universe. A sample is drawn from the universe and observations, e.g. lengths of life of electric light bulbs, are made on the units contained in the sample. The sample is assessed and inferences are made from it with regard to the universe as a whole. This procedure

175

of sampling and inferring is followed for one or more of the following reasons:

(a) The universe is infinite (or virtually infinite) in size or scope (the manufacturer of electric light bulbs may produce millions in a year).

(b) The universe is inaccessible as a whole (to carry out a market research investigation on every individual in the United Kingdom would be a physical impossibility).

(c) To sample the complete universe would destroy it (electric light bulbs are destroyed by testing for length of life).

(d) The cost of a complete enumeration would not be economically justified with respect to the value of the information obtained (if it were desired to establish whether or not the average length of life of the light bulbs were 1,500 hours, there would normally be a limit to the amount of money it would be worth expending to establish this fact, linked to the purpose for which the information was required).

The efficacy of a sampling procedure must depend upon the representative nature of the sample. Basically, and unless it is stated to the contrary, a representative sample is a random sample, by which is meant that every unit in the universe has the same chance of appearing in the sample. It is simple to state this definition, but often rather more difficult to implement it in the sampling operation itself. But, assuming this is so, then the characteristics of the sample can be related to the characteristics of the universe in a defined manner, albeit on a probability basis.

Consider, as a simplified illustration, tossing a fair penny 12 times and counting the number of heads that occur. Experience suggests that the 13 possible results, namely 0, 1, 2, . . . 11, 12 heads, are not all equally likely to occur. If you don't believe this statement, ask any gambler if he would give the same odds on all the 13 results. If the experiment (of tossing the penny 12 times) were carried through just once it would be impossible to predict the outcome precisely. There are 13 possibilities, all of which could occur, but only one actually will occur. The outcome could, however, be predicted in the shape of odds, i.e. likelihood of each possible outcome. For this particular experiment, these have been calculated (the details need not be given here) to two decimal places and are as follows:

Number of heads	0	1	2	3	4	5	6	7	8	9	10	11	12
Probability	·00	·00	·02	·06	·12	·19	·22	·19	·12	·06	·02	·00	·00

If the experiment were repeated many times, the relative frequencies with which the 13 possible results occurred would approximate to those shown in the second line of the table. Clearly, if the experiment is done once or twice only, this cannot be so, but as the number of trials gets larger and larger, the proportions observed of the different results will come closer and closer to those shown.

Now suppose alternatively that, instead of a fair penny being tossed 12 times, a fair six-sided die were tossed 12 times and the number of sixes counted. Calculations show that the revised table of probabilities will be:

Number of sixes	0	1	2	3	4	5	6	7 or over
Probability	0·11	0·26	0·30	0·20	0·09	0·03	0·01	0·00

Comparison of this table with the previous one shows quite a different pattern, and it is precisely this difference which enables inference to take place. Suppose, rather unusually, that it was not known whether a penny or a die were being tossed. The result was merely quoted as: "in a single experiment of 12 tosses, 2 successes were obtained out of the 12 tosses." Now if it were the penny, the result, although technically possible, would be a very unlikely one. Hence in the absence of any prior knowledge of the likelihood of its being the penny rather than the dice, the result of the experiment would throw heavy support behind its being the latter. Of course, if there were some prior information that the item being tossed was more likely to be one rather than the other this would, for any given experimental result, change the odds one way or the other.

B.3 The Accuracy of a Proportion

Experiments along the lines described in the previous section will show that if there is a large drum containing a very large number of beads of which a proportion p are red and the rest are blue, then in samples of size n drawn from this drum, the observed proportion of red beads in the sample will vary from sample to sample. This observed proportion will average out to p in a long run of samples, but the individual sample red bead proportions vary a lot. This variation is not completely haphazard, however, and it will be found that the sample results are almost invariably contained between

$$p - 2\sqrt{\left(\frac{p(1-p)}{n}\right)} \quad \text{and} \quad p + 2\sqrt{\left(\frac{p(1-p)}{n}\right)}$$

To illustrate this, suppose $p = 0.3$ and $n = 100$. Then the limits are

$$0.3 - 2\sqrt{\frac{0.3 \times 0.7}{100}} \quad \text{and} \quad 0.3 + 2\sqrt{\frac{0.3 \times 0.7}{100}}$$

or $\qquad$ 0·21 $\qquad$ and $\qquad$ 0·39

Hence, an individual sample drawn from such a drum, would be very unlikely to show a proportion of red beads outside the range 0·21 to 0·39.

The results may also be used the other way round. The households in a random sample of 100 from amongst all London households are approached and asked whether they intend to purchase a dishwasher in the next 12 months. 30 reply yes. Then the likely range of proportion of "yes" answers in the whole population, had every household been asked, is 0·21 to 0·39. Such an interval is termed a confidence interval. This may or may not be precise enough for the purpose in hand. If it is not, then further samples would have to be taken, but it is better to know the likely range of accuracy than to pretend that the proportion is exactly 0·3. Note that if 1,000 households had been approached and 300 reply yes (the same proportion as before) the confidence interval, following the same calculation, narrows to the band 0·27 to 0·33. The greater the size of the sample, the narrower in general will be the confidence interval.

B.4   The Interpretation of a Sampling Distribution

As a rather different illustration of how a sample result can give confidence in the result for a whole universe, consider the use of the following procedure to estimate the value of a large engineering spare parts store.

From lists it was known that 5,128 different commodities were stocked, with holdings at any one moment of time ranging from zero items to several thousand items. A random sample of 571 commodities was taken from the store, the holdings counted, and the value of each commodity obtained as the product holding times the price per unit. These values were added up for the 571 commodities and the total thus obtained multiplied by 5,128/571 to estimate the overall value of the store. This overall value came to be £46,000 (all overall values are rounded to the nearest thousand).

Now the sampling procedure used here amounted (in a slightly simplified way) to having 5,128 numbered but otherwise identical tickets in a box thoroughly mixed and drawing out 571 of them. Now suppose that this sample of tickets were replaced, the tickets were remixed and a second sample of 571 tickets drawn out. The estimate of the overall value of the store obtained from following up the commodities denoted by this second sample of tickets would most likely be different from that obtained with the first sample. Suppose further that this procedure of replacing the sample tickets and re-sampling were to be repeated a number of times. The estimated total store value would vary from occasion to occasion and the results might well take the form shown in Figure B.1, where each dot represents the result obtained from a single sampling process (the values being rounded to the nearest £2,000 for purposes of presentation). The results show, from 34 completely separate samplings, one value at £36,000, one value at £38,000, three values at £40,000, and so on up to one value at £54,000. Immediately certain features stand out. First the store values obtained by such a procedure do not roam over the whole spectrum of theoretically possible values; they are concentrated in a band of values. Secondly, even within the defined band, the values are more likely at the centre and fall away in likelihood at the two extremes, so that 18 out of 34 (or

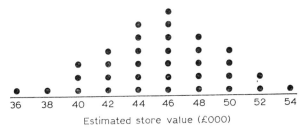

Figure B.1 Distribution of sample estimates

53%) of the values are either £44,000, £46,000 or £48,000, and only 3 out of 34 (9%) are as much as £8,000 above or below the central peak at £46,000.

Extending the above approach, if a very large number of samples were similarly taken, store values estimated from each but not rounded off, and plotted as in Figure B.1, the outline of the distribution thus formed would be along the line shown in Figure B.2, curve A. This sampling distribution, so-called, of an estimated total value will, for all practical purposes, always have the characteristic symmetrical bell-shaped outline shown. The shape or form of the distribution is referred to as the "Normal" or "Gaussian" distribution. Such a distribution is characterized by two values: the mean or average value which will fall at the point of symmetry, and the standard deviation which is a statistical measure of the spread of the distribution. The range (i.e. the highest minus the lowest value) of the distribution is approximately four standard deviations for this case of some thirty observations, so that a spread from £36,000 to £54,000 suggests a standard deviation of $\frac{1}{4}(54,000 - 36,000)$, or £4,500. Curve B shows another Normal distribution with a narrower spread than curve A; the standard deviation in this instance would probably be around £3,000, or about two-thirds that of curve A. The practical implication is that an estimated total value having sampling distribution B will have a greater chance of being within a defined amount from the true (but unknown) total than one with sampling distribution A. Differences in standard deviation can arise from a

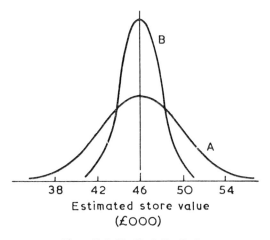

Figure B.2 Idealized distribution

number of sources, but in the present instance the most likely source would be the size of the sample—the larger the sample used the smaller would be the standard deviation of the sampling distribution.

Extensive tables of areas of the Normal distribution are available in terms of multiples of the standard deviation (s.d.) For example, extracts from the tables give the following:

50% of sample results are obtained within the band defined by mean ±0·67 s.d.
80% of sample results are obtained within the band defined by mean ±1·28 s.d.
90% of sample results are obtained within the band defined by mean ±1·64 s.d.
95% of sample results are obtained within the band defined by mean ±1·96 s.d.

B.5   The Confidence Interval

From the foregoing it is seen that the smaller the standard deviation the greater the chance that the value estimated from the sample is near the true value. Using tables of the Normal distribution it is possible to be rather more precise than this and to give confidence intervals as done previously for proportions. The following example illustrates what is meant:

"There is a 95% chance that the true total value is within the range:
estimated total value ± 1·96 × standard deviation."

The beauty of this approach is that, provided the sampling method used is basically a random method, it is possible to estimate the standard deviation of the sampling distribution from the sample itself. Hence even though only a single sample (consisting of a number of units) is taken, some idea of the possible range of the true unknown value is possible. Suppose, therefore, that a sample estimate of a store value gave an estimated value of £42,500 and an estimated standard deviation of £2,300. This could then be interpreted as meaning that there is a 95% chance that the true total value is within the range £42,500 ± £4,554 (or £38,000 to £47,000). If this is not accurate enough for the purpose in hand, it will be necessary to devise a sampling method giving a smaller standard deviation, but to do so may well mean that some extra cost will be incurred.

Index

Ackoff, R. L., 17
Advertising media problem, 135
Allocation of funds, 133
Analogue model, 9, 152
Analytic methods, 155
A priori probabilities, 115
Assignment problems, 34

Basic feasible solution, 169
Battersby, A., 32, 108
Baumol, W. J., 61
Bayes, Thomas, 115
Beale, E. M. L., 61, 136, 150, 173, 174
Beer, Stafford, 90, 166
Bellman, R., 173, 174
Boiler installation problem, 112 ff.
Bottlenecks, 65 ff.
Boulding, K. E., 48
Brain centre concept, 164
Bross, I. D. J., 127
Brown, R. G., 108

Camp, G. D., 153
Capital budgeting, 132
Chambers, D. J., 132, 150
Checking invoices, 147
Chemical company new plant problem, 118
Chernoff, H., 127
Churchman, C. W., 108
Clothing industry, 134
Coaker, G., 4
Colchester Post Office, 75
Composite working, 74
Confidence interval, 178, 180
Constant cycle system, 105
Constraints, 36 ff., 52, 133
Constraints, relaxation, 42
Construction of a house, 23
Contour lines, 41
Cox, D. R., 76

Critical path, 22
Critical path analysis, *see* Network analysis
Cunard Steam-Ship Company, 161

Dantzig, G. B., 48, 174
Dearden, J., 90
Decision trees, 120 ff.
Deckling problem, 55 ff.
Duckworth, W. E., 17
Dummy event, 22
Dynamic programming, 173

E.M.V., 118 ff.
Ellis, D. M., 135, 150
Erlang, K., 64
Event times, 24
Everclear Plastics Company, 138
Expected values, 115 ff.
Exponential forecasting, 108

Fishburn, P. C., 127
Fisons Company, 161
Float, 23, 25
Flow diagram for rolling mill problem, 85 ff.
Flow diagram for ship unloading, 14
Forecasting, analogue model for, 9
Forecasting return on capital investment, 116
Form and content, 15
Forrester, J. W., 90, 103, 108
Frequency distributions, 79 ff.

Gass, S. I., 48
Gaussian distribution, 179
General allocation problem, 34
Gilbert, W. S., 1
Green, P. E., 138, 151

Hadley, G., 173
Handling equipment problem, 49

Harrogate Head Post Office, 74
Harvey, W. S., 57, 61
Hotel, fitting out, 31

IPA/NRS survey, 136
Iconic models, 152
Implementation of a study, 12, 157 ff.
Integer programming, 173
Inventory, 91 ff.
  buffer stock, 97 ff.
  carrying cost, 92
  centralized stores, 100
  control systems, 105
  feedback control, 106
  re-order cost, 93
  re-order level, 96
  safety stock, 99
Invoices, checking of, 147
Iso-profit lines, 173

Jowett, E., 57, 61

Kirkpatrick, C. A., 48
Kromel plastic, 138

Land Commission, establishment of, 28
Levin, R. I., 48
Linearity, 47
Linear programming, 36 ff.
Local Government Operational Research Unit, 148
Location of factory, analogue model for, 10
Location problem, 128 ff.
Lockyer, K. G., 32
Lottery, 115

Machine loss coefficient, 72
Machine servicing, 69 ff.
Magee, J. F., 108, 127
Marginal analysis, 42
Matrix, 168 ff.
Maximin decision rule, 110
McFarlan, F. W., 90
Merrett, A. J., 113
Minimax regret rule, 110
Minimum cost problem, 44
Model-building, 88
Models, types of, 7
Monte Carlo technique, 79 ff.
Morse, P. M., 76
Moses, L. E., 127
Muth, J. F., 32

National Economic Development Council, 134
Negative exponential distribution, 65
Network analysis
  analysing the network, 20, 25
  construction of house, 23
  costs, 31
  drawing the network, 21
  dummy event, 23
  event times, 24
  financial incentives, 18
  float, 23, 25
  illustrations, 28 ff.
  preparing the network, 20
  published examples, 19
Non-certainty, 16
Normal distribution, 179
Numerical methods, 155

Operation of systems, 5
Operational Research, definition of, 2
Operational Research, phases of a study, 11
Operational Research Society, 2, 162
  membership of, 161
Opportunity profit, 169
Organization and Methods, 163
Outcome matrix, 165

Page, A. C. C., 17, 85, 90
Paine, N. R., 61
Palm, C., 69, 76
Paper-making problem, 55 ff.
PERT, *see* Network analysis
Pivot, 169
Pivotal row, column, 169
Port, unloading, 85 ff.
Post Office counter problem, 74 ff.
Preference curve, 125
Pricing problem, 138
Probability theory, 78
Problem definition, 11
Proportion, accuracy of, 177
Pseudo-random numbers, 83

Quadratic programming, 173
Queue discipline, 84
Queueing, 62 ff.

RAMPS, *see* Network analysis
Random numbers, 82 ff.
Random sample, 81 ff.
Relaxation of constraints, 42
Re-order level, 106

Re-order quantity, 106
Repairmen Loss Coefficient, 72
Risk, 16
Risk aversion, 125
Rivett, B. H. P., 17, 162
Role of operational research, 160
Rolling mill problem, 83 ff.
Rugby Portland Cement Co., 161
Ryan, W. S., 32

Sample, 175
Sasieni, M., 76
Schlaifer, R., 125, 127
Scientific method, adaptation, 7
Shipping channel illustration, 13
Simplex method, 49, 167 ff.
Simulation, 77 ff., 102, 156
Slide rule, 152
Smith, W. H. & Son Ltd., 161
Smith, W. L., 76
Spivey, W. A., 48
Square-root formula, 91 ff.
Standard deviation, 179
Steer, D. T., 17, 85, 90
Stock control, *see* Inventory
Supermarket, 62, 67
Swimming-pool problem, 109
Sykes, A., 113
Symbolic models, 8, 152

Team approach, 3
Team working, 74

Thompson, G. L., 32
Tocher, K. D., 90
Traffic intensity, 64 ff.
Transportation problem, 3, 35
Transrad Company, 36
Tree diagram, 143
Trigg, D. W., 108
Tull, D. S., 117, 127, 138, 151
Two-bin stock system, 105

Uncertainty, 16
United Steel Company, 161
Universe, 175
Unloading problem, 85 ff.
Utility, 125
Utility curve, 125

Vajda, S., 61, 173
Verlon plastic, 138

Waiting-line, *see* Queueing
Ward, R. A., 148, 151
Wardle, P. A., 61
Weighted average, 115
Welch, W. E., 108
Wiggins Teape Co., 57, 59
Williams, J. D., 127
Williams, N., 61
Wolfe, P., 61, 173
Work study, 163